THE IMPOSSIBLE DREAM

The Story of the Miracle Boston Red Sox

by Bill McSweeny

THE IMPOSSIBLE DREAM

VIOLENCE EVERY SUNDAY (*with Mike Holovak*)

GO UP FOR GLORY (*with Bill Russell*)

THE

The Story of the

BILL McSWEENY

IMPOSSIBLE DREAM

Miracle Boston Red Sox

ILLUSTRATED WITH PHOTOGRAPHS

Coward-McCann, Inc.
New York

Library of Congress Catalog Card Number: 68-22320

PRINTED IN THE UNITED STATES OF AMERICA
BY THE COLONIAL PRESS INC.
CLINTON, MASSACHUSETTS

This saga of a baseball team which ranged from the sublime to the courageous to the ridiculous can truly have only one dedication:

To the long-suffering members of the Boston Chapter of the Baseball Writers of America, who proved their class, win or lose.

And as a personal aside, to these forgotten men in aging Red Sox grays who spent all those years on the sandlots looking honestly for talent, and who were major-leaguers all the way: Ernest Stevens, Al Morelli, and their batboys, Chuckie Morelli and Billy McSweeny III.

And, of course, to the enduring mascot, Cathy.

Foreword

In the course of twenty-five years, I have benefited by—and bitten nails raw in the course of—some of the best assignments any man has ever had.

This assignment has been the most difficult. The Impossible Dream is the dream of every man. In 1967, the Red Sox somehow put together the pieces of countless egos, twenty-five playing talents and four men in a front office, and achieved something which captured our imagination.

In recounting their story, the first feeling was that it should be honest, so that those who treasure their story will also understand the past history, the weaknesses and the strengths of a team and a game which has often gone awry. Many of us grew up believing baseball to be all honesty and courage in the clutch. To write in that vein would be to dishonor the things which are good about the 1967 Red Sox, the human element which makes it all the more believable and real to those of us who only watch and vicariously participate.

Baseball is no better than life. If, as its flacks claim, baseball is truly our national pastime and if sports are characteristic of our people, then baseball and the culture of America must both be held accountable in future generations.

There have been good moments in the sport and there

have been bad, just as the men themselves have been good and bad, or uncaring and unkind.

Finally, it became apparent that the only way to tell this full story was to range across the entire spectrum of what the Red Sox have been and leave judgments to those who may wish to make them. In certain places the Brahmins of baseball will screech. This is the normal reaction of persons pricked in a conscience influenced by gate receipts, television monies and the number of men, women and children who huddle eating green hot dogs on cold rainy spring or fall days, dreaming their own impossible dreams and seeing small, personal evidences of it on green fields.

It is a toy world and a toy game. Compared to a battalion of airborne troopers who this day achieved the heights of a hill near Dak To, South Vietnam, the accomplishments are very small indeed.

But it is all part of us. The Red Sox date back to the beginning of this century. They have been part of our national sport in good times and in bad—and have evidenced throughout each period one small indication of what our culture is, was, or will be.

This is their story, from the beginning to the end in 1967. It is, finally, just the story of men, doing their best, or their least, for money, while in pursuit of fame . . . and money.

It was not until 1943 that I was first permitted in the Red Sox dugout—and then only to carry photo plates—and throughout a varied ensuing career I saw baseball and the team through a different position than most sportswriters.

This book is an attempt to call the shot as objectively as possible over the whole wide spectrum. It is written alone, not because I do not have faith in other writers, but because I wish to make it clear to any who may have complaints that the facts as I know—and have researched—them to be are my facts. Baseball writers have a tough enough job as it is without having anyone—owner, general manager, manager or player—take my words and reports out on them.

Baseball writing is both a chore and a joy. As a kid, my greatest dream was to become a baseball writer. As the years went on, everyone came to know it was the most difficult physical assignment, the most demanding—and, occasionally, drunken—task in the profession of reporting sports.

I cannot commend this book to anyone. But I can commend to the reader about 90 percent of the baseball writers in this country. The other 10 percent are of a type which is just the normal law of averages in any business.

The game? The impossible dream? That you must take as you find it.

In life or in the toy world of baseball.

BILL McSWEENY

Boston
November 24, 1967

Contents

1. THE NEW BREED 15
2. THE OLD BREED 24
3. THE SPORTSMAN 39
4. THE LEAGUE PRESIDENT 53
5. WILLIAMS THE FIRST 60
6. THE COUNTRY CLUB 82
7. WILLIAMS THE SECOND 132
8. THE YEAR OF THE YAZ 153
9. THE GREAT FLOUNDER 178
10. THE WAITING TIME 192
11. THE MONEY GAMES 199
12. EL BIRDOS 213
13. THE WORLD SERIES 219
14. EPILOGUE 234

APPENDIX 247

THE IMPOSSIBLE DREAM

The Story of the Miracle Boston Red Sox

1.

The New Breed

IT WAS, of course, an impossible dream. The Red Sox were not going to win the pennant in 1967 and everyone knew it. Baseball has had its wild groups, the Gas House Gang of the old Cardinals for representation of one phase and the Brooklyn Dodgers for a more modern period.

They boozed a lot. It was said, even, that they occasionally chased skirts and played cards for high stakes. Once, it was even mentioned that some didn't even remember church on Sundays. But this, of course, was probably because they were so intent on arriving at the ball park early.

Dark rumors said that the 1940s-1950s Yankees, while more austere in their nightly travails (after all you can't even start a fistfight in the Copa without being in business suit and tie), also had their moments and their playboys.

No one denied that the same was so of the Red Sox.

The difference was that the old Cards and Dodgers and Yankees won pennants and world championships. Ice-cold towels on the neck in the dugout and black coffee and an aspirin in the training room, perhaps. But still, for the big ones, they were the money players.

The Red Sox? Oh, that was so much different. After all, it wasn't how you played the game really. Not really. It was how you conned whatever manager happened to be there at the time; how you conned whoever was the poor fall guy sitting in the general manager's box and sweating. And most important of all, how you conned Mr. Yawkey.

He was Mr. Yawkey to most, T.A. to a privileged executive few, and Tom to a Boston press who used the familiar in fairly unfamiliar circumstances, because for years he never posed for a picture and gave extraordinarily few press conferences; except once or twice when he was furious and stormed into the press room to blow his top, plowing out of there again in a wake of retainers who knew better, but said, "Right, T.A."

On the basis of all that, everyone just *knew* the Red Sox weren't going to win any pennant in 1967. I mean, baseball wasn't the grand old game anymore, anyway. Politicians, poltroons and powerful business interests had long since changed it into the grand old shell game and a probably-nice-man named William D. Eckert was the Commissioner of Baseball, his old Air Force General's stars long since in storage and tarnishing; taking orders like a corporal from his twenty bosses and shepherded everywhere by old A.P. wise-baseball-writer Joe Reichler. The Commissioner looked frightened when Reichler wasn't there, almost, as someone said, as though he was afraid some wise guy might ask him to point out first base.

Baseball had fallen far, ebbing out on a fast tide while the new and slicker wave of pro football washed in. The new owners could count return on investment fast. Sport? Forget it. The few remaining old owners—who could handle money pretty good themselves—were said to be fading from power.

Yawkey? Who was he? A senior owner, in fact the senior owner in his league. A spender, sure. In the vernacular of the trade he "sent it in" pretty good, spoiling some potentially exceptional players, pouring it over Ted Williams like it was so much honey to keep a grumpy bee happy, wasting it in gigantic proportions on bonus players who couldn't hit a lick and were Blue Cross cases in the field; playing favorites with young kids whose heads were easily turned and with ex-players who caught the brass ring of a soft touch in the front office.

It had long since become a joke. The joint was a country club. Everyone knew that, from the best, most aggressive scout who found a home and became lazy; to the worst of the drunks who lugged into the best touch in sports and suffered watching a game only to get back to the free bar.

In baseball, everyone knew it figured. Talent isn't enough. It takes, as some broad in a musical said, heart. This might not be the year the Yankees won the pennant, but it certainly wasn't going to be the year the Red Sox won it.

It was as simple as the law of gravity. The Red Sox would go up fast and then, wham, they would come down. In February and March, it would be first division and pennant talk. In April, they would promise to "win more than we lose." In May, they would make an interesting swing out on the road, win a few home games, excite the crowd briefly early in June and then settle to their own level, sometimes last and sometimes next to last and even occasionally actually getting into the first division.

The first division? The Red Sox thought that was something in the Army. And not too many of them were anxious to get involved in *that*. Uh-uh. Play it safe and loose. And who cared anyway?

Old T. A. Yawkey was just a nice guy who was orphaned young and raised by an uncle who owned the Detroit Tigers. He was just a real nice guy that liked to play pepper, wearing his Red Sox suit in that real pretty, small ball yard with nobody watching; just playing better pepper than some of the clubhouse hangers-on, who knew better than to play pepper better than Mr. Yawkey.

Nice guy, T.A., old Tom, Mr. Yawkey. The money is good, the years go by. He shows up in late spring to watch awhile and then goes away again finally, leaving his digs at the Ritz Carlton for a fling, maybe, with Horace Stoneham of the New York-San Francisco Giants at the Pierre; then taking off to his place in the Carolinas to shoot off his repressions against pheasants. "Oh well," they all said, "old Yawkey can afford it. He owns half the lumber in the world and God knows what else. He burned himself out rooting for his boy, Ted Williams, and the best team in baseball back in the late forties; except that they never had the heart to win but one pennant and they staggered into that down the stretch in 1946."

So, most certainly, this wasn't going to be the year the Red Sox won the pennant. It was going to be just exactly like every other year.

Everyone *knew* that.

Except a small handful. Yawkey. The general manager, Dick O'Connell, who had finally finessed his way through more intrigues than Machiavelli to gain some semblance of control. Haywood Sullivan, the director of player personnel, only a so-so major league catcher but an old Southern horse-trader with players. And this new guy, Dick Williams, the manager—*the* manager—but only in on a one-year contract and just glad to have one shot at the big leagues, a money shot, make-or-break, and if he blew it, so what the hell, at least there would be a major league coaching job somewhere.

If you put all four together in April just before they split from the training camp at Winter Haven, Florida, and asked them to bet something serious on the pennant there would have been no takers. But for the first time in oh-so-long—and, God, it really was that long, wasn't it?—there was the slimmest possible chance that they really would win more than they would lose.

The Minnesota Twins were the class of the league. No doubt of that, whether a good manager, Sam Mele, was having trouble with front office fatheads or some lardheads who were becoming too big league to play as they were told.

Eddie Stanky had Chicago's White Sox. Cops told you that you'd take your life in your hands to go out to that old ball park in Chi, and around the league they said Stanky used that to scare other teams as much as anything. His team couldn't hit a lick. His team couldn't play the game like the American League designed it to be played. But Stanky—darn that Stanky—came from the National League and he'd con you and scare you to death and run and beat you by 2-1.

In the old days—and days not that very far past—it was said that bored Red Sox managers fell asleep in the dugout. It was said more privately than publicly. And it was true. I mean, how excited can you get fighting to keep half a game out of ninth place?

So, Stanky could be counted on to do away with sleep and he was a contender too, more on brazen corn and con. But, a contender.

And, at last, Detroit finally had a team which could do it. As long as Kaline stayed well they could do it easily.

So the small handful of four men who had the dream faced the reality that, in honesty, it would be impossible. In Vegas and in Minneapolis, where unemotional men who understand the uses of money and odds established the line, there was complete agreement that the Red Sox were impossible.

Jimmy "the Greek" Snyder made it a 100-to-1 shot, a far-back grouping just to entice any sucker money. *Nobody* bets on the Red Sox. Not to win a pennant. And in Vegas some New England businessman, trying his luck at the tables, surprised himself and won a hundred. Easy come, easy go. For a lark he put it down on Boston at 100-to-1. He *knew* he wouldn't win. After all, he was an old Red Sox fan. He'd been there before, too. But it's Vegas. Take a lark with a sure loser.

In the spring training camp at Winter Haven, the atmosphere was almost the same. The new manager, Williams, was not unknown to the Boston press. He had been a journeyman player, whiling some time away with the Red Sox, neither popular nor unpopular. Just another guy. It was said he had done well with the International League farm team in Toronto. But Toronto wasn't the big leagues. And he was strange, this Williams. Crazy things, like umpiring behind the plate to watch the pitchers. Like giving fresh answers to stupid questions, but never playing the press off one against another and developing self-protective cliques, previously a must for a Red Sox manager.

Williams was actually being the boss, bringing in Bobby Doerr as his first-base coach. Doerr, the captain of the last pennant winner, was a class guy, slow-talking, still shy as he approached middle age. Public relations-wise, it was a good move. But, who the heck was this fellow Eddie Popowski, who'd never been west of the Eastern League and whose biggest dream was to see Disneyland on the first swing out to Anaheim? Fifty years old and never in the big leagues, player or manager. Just another minor league manager, driving the bus, counseling the kids, mad at them sometimes and not letting them even have a watering stop for aching kidneys if they didn't play well and lost a game. A minor league manager, looking funny in his Red Sox hat. What was this Williams using him for? A clown prince? Was he running a gag?

In on only a one-year contract and even that a shock. Everyone knew that Billy Herman would get a new contract with the Sox for 1967. It figured as just a routine announcement late in the 1966 season. Writers straggled into Fenway to listen to the same old song. Herman wasn't a bad manager and a couple of times he made it exciting, vital, even clawed his way into the first division before the bottom finally fell out.

But then, suddenly G.M. O'Connell—he of the soft voice, of patience, determination; a guy who took the raps and kept his mouth shut, who watched the front office politickers come and go, surviving it all on equal shares of integrity and plain common sense—stood up and said:

"It pains me to make this announcement. We have decided to make a change."

And now, here in the big leagues, was Williams. Everywhere. Scrambling. Umpiring. Arguing. Demanding that players be in shape. Making some hate him and some love him and already having some of his players say that he played favorites:

"Do good for him, he smiles at you. He loves you. He's with you. Go hitless six games and he doesn't know your name."

Angry at him, this usurper of their peaceful club. A run-down ex-journeyman ballplayer trying to be boss.

All season long they would have trouble with him. Some of them would never understand him. Some would wind up winning the pennant and hating him. Some would privately predict that he would never be able to win another one.

But, this was his year and his time and his place, into the command position of a major league team. Short money, sure. About $22,000—never owned a house in his life; renting furniture for his apartment in Boston's distant suburb of Peabody.

But, up there nevertheless. And the deal had been made long before that September noon near the end of the 1966 season when O'Connell said, "We have decided to make a change."

It had been made, in fact, in June, before Herman—in the second and final year of his contract—actually made a run at Orioles, so proudly going for it all in the year they would win it. Herman, good guy, very nice man, ace bridge player, well liked by most of the press and sort of a tolerated paterfamilias to some of his players—neither hated nor loved, in fact not even arousing any seething emotion which must go with a team with spirit—yes, Herman was gone. He didn't know it.

But Williams knew it in Toronto. Yawkey and O'Connell and Sullivan knew it at Fenway.

Because it had to be that way. A lot of the weeds had been yanked from the garden spot. There were a couple of new kids who actually had desire to go with their talent. Another young one who had been so confused, so temperamental, had finally been guided, aided and basically straightened out.

It was hard to pin it down. But there was, somehow, at least the basic element of the New Breed, a name which is more directly associated with the Marines of Korea and Vietnam. Ordinarily it would be an insult, particularly in this time of war, death, rubber-packing bags and aluminum coffins, even to attempt to compare basically draft-dodging Reservist-Guardsmen ("And, oh don't bother to show up Sunday, Charlie, I know you're playing") with the young ones who 12,000 miles away put it on a different line.

But it was the New Breed; at least the beginning of it and as the year went on, as they finally became a team and fought for it, floundered, fought for it again and then pulled it out, this one small team of 25 players captured the imagination of an entire nation and for that long, staggering, soaring month of September and the stretched seven games of the World Series, each in his own way somehow took professional baseball out of the cashier's cage and away from CBS and made it again the crystal-clear dream.

So this is the opening of its story. One year, one club—finally one capable opponent—and the persons who made it all tick. A writer would be a liar, perhaps even worse, to attempt to make them more giant than life, because they were not. A man would be unfaithful to his code to shield the bad parts and tell only the good. The only way to tell it really is to include the bad and the good, the intrigues and ineptitudes, the planning, the luck, the failures, the misunderstanding and the misunderstood.

For one small period, one microscopic spasm, it worked.

The culture of the nation would not change, nor its policies and its wars. Yet something, some intangible, however brief, was restored for us here; perhaps only to be remembered finally as the year when, in winning it, the Red Sox took the minds of people off war, politics, troubles and at the same time saved baseball from completely becoming a grubby, dollar-chasing farce devoted to the whims of television sponsors, aggressive executives with three-button suits just a little too sharp, and sundry camp followers and fringe hucksters who were making it all a complete fraud.

Three front office men and a manager signed for one year with no guarantees and a squad of individualists who couldn't have cared less for a team.

Then, suddenly, it was spring training at Winter Haven. The country club began to fade. The best in men began to come out.

2.

The Old Breed

IF ONE is to understand why the Red Sox were able to capture our imagination in 1967 it is necessary to recount their antecedents. Stengel and the Yankees will probably be the remembered dynasty a hundred years from now—if anyone bothers to remember baseball at all. The owners, the hustlers and the rubber-stamp commissioners have taken a good part of the legend and reduced it to public relations hash. In the old days—those desperately lovely days when people believed one war would end them all; when women were ladies and families didn't have to be exhorted to pray together—in those old days there was still something beautiful about baseball.

There were hustlers then as well, on the field and in the front office, but television and modern living and the massive growth of other professional sports hadn't come along to show baseball up for what it has become. Inside us, the older ones, the middle generation, there was still the twinge of memory of what it was when we were young. The Red Sox restored a little credence to the money game by winning the pennant in 1967. Some of the color came back and when it finally turned out to be the Red Sox, well, to a lot of people there was at least an association with the old days. After all, no matter how old you may be, there always was a Red Sox team. In some periods it was a pretty fascinating one at that.

In fact, it is most remarkable that so much baseball has revolved around the Red Sox. Connie Mack helped found them. A tough kid named Babe Ruth pitched for them. Jim Lonborg would win the Cy Young Award in 1967. And who did Cy Young pitch for? The Red Sox, of course. What was the greatest outfield? Speaker-Hooper-Lewis, experts said. And a fan from Lawrence contributed something to baseball called "Casey at the Bat."

Yes, Boston was always a baseball town. When it became time to hustle cities by moving franchises—why, naturally, where did it first happen? Boston. Lou Perini took the Braves to Milwaukee so quickly that his local spokesmen were still denying the move while the team was headed there. Expansion was on, the great race for the money—most of which they claim Walter O'Malley got in Los Angeles—and Boston had contributed one more chapter to the grand old game; the grand old shell game.

Somehow, the Red Sox themselves have always managed to be a slightly better symbol. Even in bad years (and they had plenty of these). Perhaps, it just comes from at least staying in the same city.

The Red Sox were born as the Boston Puritans on May 8, 1901, something which sometimes gave observers of the modern Sox a chuckle. During their "country club" days anyone with an old memory would smile. "Puritans. Imagine these guys being grandsons of the Puritans."

Boston had been a National League monopoly for 25 years before this sudden intrusion. Indeed, the National League team (now the Boston-Milwaukee-Atlanta Braves) were called the Red Stockings.

Using Connie Mack to lease ground for a field on Huntington Avenue, American League President Ban Johnson struck quickly. Before the National League knew exactly what was happening, the Boston Puritans were in action with as player-manager the first of the "jumpers," third baseman Jimmy Collins, who was signed away from the Red Stockings. Collins appears to have been a born wheeler-dealer. He picked up Cy Young from the Cardinals for a salary of $3,500 and also grabbed off his battery mate, Lou Criger. The result was the first pennant in 1903, when the Puritans beat Mack's Athletics by sixteen and a half games and then defeated the Pirates 5-3 in the first World Series.

It just figured that nothing Boston did would come easily. The historical mansion of major league baseball has many hidden rooms, some of which will never come to light, although Bill Veeck did make a startling discovery behind an old table in a storeroom under the park when he had the White Sox, finding a notebook which indicated there was more than just the Black Sox scandal in baseball's early, shady past.

There also were cliques which owned two, three and four clubs (hence Philadelphia Mack's interest in leasing the original field for Boston). That isn't unknown in the growth days of other professional sports operations, either.

The Boston Puritans' trouble in '03 was basic—greed. Even the press was forced to buy tickets for admission. Nothing—absolutely nothing—can cause a bigger beef stew than charging a reporter for his seat. There also was some complaint about double ticket sales. The Red Sox had a pennant and a World Series and a theme song—some strange chant called "Tessie" which still is heard every now and again. They also had troubles. President Johnson, a clever man growing stronger (until Landis and the owners finally eliminated him after the Black Sox scandal), directed that Boston be sold to someone more reputable.

In 1904 the team was purchased by General Charles Taylor of the Boston *Globe*. His son, John, directed his interests. Over the next six years Boston kept building up. A good catcher from Holy Cross, Bill Carrigan, came aboard in '06, the National League dropped Red Stockings in '07 and the Boston Red Sox were officially named and in the same year a young kid from the Texas league named Tristram Speaker was purchased for $750. Someone who would become famous as Smokey Joe Wood was bought from Kansas City and Harry Hooper traveled in from Sacramento in 1908. In 1909, Duffy Lewis was signed from Oakland, thus creating the most famous outfield of its generation—Hooper, Lewis and Speaker.

By 1912, Taylor sold 50 percent back to Johnson's men and Fenway Park—the same park of this 1967 impossible dream—was built.

Dry history? I don't think so. The glory of their times. The glory of pre-World War I America. It was the only sport that counted. Everyone played baseball and the sport of 1967 was being shaped by the events of these years. It had its characters, its moments of greatness, its legendary errors and, as well, its robber barons. Why should it not? Isn't baseball, in the final essence, a small cameo of the United States itself? Does it really matter that some of those who strode across this stage center were as guilty of human weaknesses as are we all?

These early years had their moments. Jimmy Collins became so sickened of managing that he staggered through a couple of seasons of quitting in midyear, returning as a private, then quit all together. Chick Stahl, the unwilling replacement skipper, committed suicide in spring training; a drinking bout at the midwinter meetings of '08-09 between the original owner, Charlie Somers, and a Red Sox official resulted in the trading to Cleveland of Cy Young for a skimpy $12,500 and two long-since-forgotten pitchers. Cliques ruined the Red Sox, with Speaker and Wood forming one publicly adored and privately detested element.

Familiar? Of course, the *human* element, as much a part then as now. The same old stories. Only the names have changed.

In 1912, the Red Sox defeated John McGraw's Giants four games to three, a World Series which required eight games, the second having ended in an eleven-inning tie. The victory in the final game came on a rally in the tenth inning when Giants' center fielder Fred Snodgrass missed an easy fly which went for a double and set the stage for the 3-2 Boston victory. Snodgrass' error was marked up as the first of baseball's famous fluffs—"Snodgrass' $30,000 muff" which was the difference between the total winning and losing team bonus.

Baseball was moving and in 1914 along came Ruth, purchased from Baltimore in a package deal with Ernie Shore for about $2,900. The legend of the man as a hitter has obscured the fact that he was also one of the great left-handed pitchers of all time who set the record of consecutive scoreless innings in a World Series with 29 2/3 innings. His runner-up was Christy Mathewson with 28 1/3.

So much has been written of Ruth that it becomes difficult to separate the legend from the man. Yet one man knew him better than most and, if we labor long on Red Sox history, it is nevertheless of more than passing interest and remarkable coincidence that a scout of the pennant-winning Red Sox in 1967 was Joe Dugan, the one man closest to Ruth through it all, from his early days to the moment they wheeled his casket down the aisle of St. Patrick's Cathedral.

He was a gargantuan man, Ruth. He made baseball. Ultimately, perhaps because of his own personality, perhaps for other reasons more sublime, he was betrayed by baseball's owners, winding up his days in 1935 as a .181 hitter with the Boston Braves.

Always, his shadow was cast over baseball. Through the 1967 pennant race and on into the World Series, one could listen to the literate, wise Dugan tell old stories. Baseball came as much alive from the shadows as from the efforts on the field of Yaz and Lonborg and Scott.

What kind of a man was he? Dugan said:

"You had to understand him like this. He was an animal. No human being could have done the things he did and lived the way he did and been the ballplayer he was. Name any of them. Cobb? Speaker? Listen, I saw them all. I was there. There was never anybody close. When you figure all the things he did then you just have to remember he wasn't human. He was a god."

This legend can be marked down as well then. Baseball, good and bad, human beings at stage center in moments of stress. Ruth and the Red Sox and a man remembered in 1967 as "an animal . . . and a god."

When Ruth came to the Red Sox, "Rough" Bill Carrigan was both his catcher and his manager. Carrigan lives the fullest of lives and still cheered the 1967 Red Sox. He may have been one of the greatest of managers. Ty Cobb told me once: "His teams never had style, but they were the hardest ones to beat. Carrigan and Ruth beat me for the pennant in 1915 and they were really good."

More on Cobb later, in modern times, because he too was a part of the Red Sox scene, most particularly in his visits to spring training camps and his friendship and final, disastrous blowup with Ted Williams. Cobb—the first man selected to the Hall of Fame—always had his own personal feud with Ruth, which extended even to the golf course, where he beat Ruth in a War Bond series, one of which was played at The Country Club in Brookline. The old man, dying now back in 1961, remembered the golf match as much as baseball, possibly because against Ruth in 1915 he wasn't able to win the pennant.

"I only beat him by outthinking him. By keeping the pressure on him. That was the only thing with the Babe. You had to pressure him into blowing up," he would say of the golf matches. "In baseball, though, you couldn't expect him to blow up under pressure. He was just superb. A superb animal."

Again, the phrase—animal. A unique distinction.

Ruth was fortunate that his first manager was Carrigan. How did he handle him?

"I roomed with him," Carrigan said. "He never gave me any trouble. You had to remember his background—that orphan asylum and all—and he never had the vaguest idea what money was all about. He'd buy anything and everything. I moved him in with me and drew his pay and put him on an allowance. At the end of the year, I'd give him his money that I'd saved. I guess it would last him a month. One thing about Ruth, though. People think when he came up to us in 1914 I sent him down to Providence for more seasoning. That wasn't exactly true. He pitched four games for us, but we were out of the race mathematically. We ended up second. That was the year the Braves made the big miracle. They were in last place in July and they went on to win the pennant and beat the A's four straight in the World Series.

"Ruth had a 2-1 record with us, but Joe Lannin, who owned the team, also owned Providence and they had a chance at the International League pennant. Lannin sent Ruth down to help and they did win the pennant. That was typical of baseball then. I guess it still is in a way," Carrigan said.

In 1915 the Red Sox had all the horses. They also had dissension. In "the greatest outfield of all time" Lewis and Speaker refused even to speak, except for a perfunctory comment on a fly ball:

"I got it."

"You take it."

Their dispute—a clash of egos long since growing—came when the team shaved its heads for an extended western trip in the blistering heat of St. Louis, a park so intensely hot that years later Red Sox scout Jack Burns would watch the 1967 Series with the Cards and say: "When I was out in St. Loo with the Browns it used to be so hot that when we came into the dugout we'd have a hole filled with water. We'd put our

Babe Ruth is shown as a Red Sox player when he was setting records for a pitcher before his hitting made him a Yankee.

Cy Young, after whom baseball's top pitching award was named, was the greatest of the early Red Sox hurlers.

Joe DiMaggio, left, and Lou Gehrig chat with Mayor Fiorello LaGuardia before meeting Cubs in the World Series.

It's a long way from Boston and the Baltimore orphanage as Babe Ruth hits his famed sixtieth homer in 1927.

This was the Babe in his prime.

Joe DiMaggio trots home after his round tripper beat the Red Sox in final pennant-at-stake games in 1950. Berra greets him.

The early Red Sox of Tom Yawkey had another great and controversial pitcher in Lefty Grove.

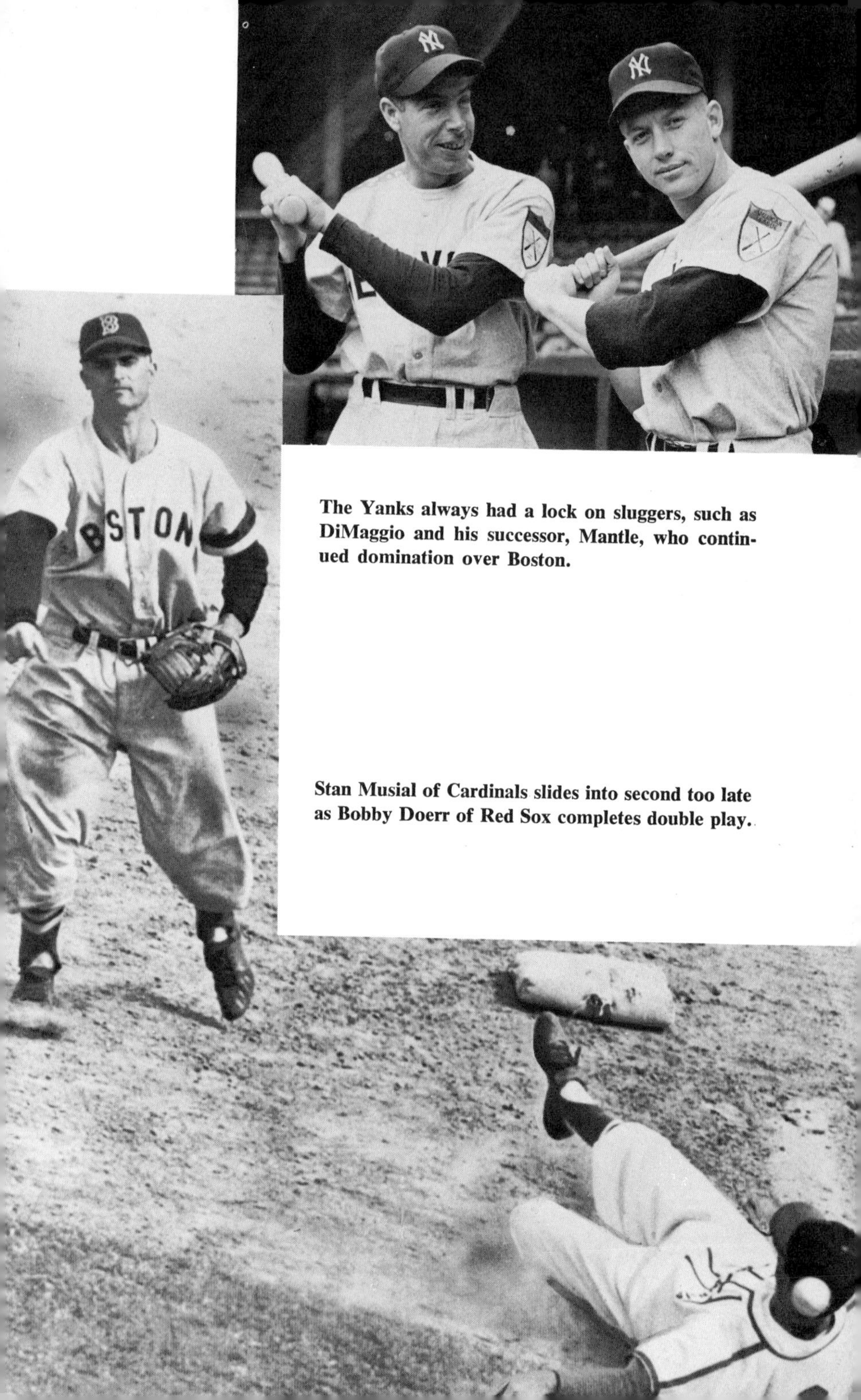

The Yanks always had a lock on sluggers, such as DiMaggio and his successor, Mantle, who continued domination over Boston.

Stan Musial of Cardinals slides into second too late as Bobby Doerr of Red Sox completes double play.

spikes in there to cool our feet off and the water would hiss and steam would come up."

The haircuts lasted only so long. Everyone's hair grew again except that of Lewis, a natty dresser who would go nattily on many years later as traveling secretary of the Boston Braves.

Lewis was most conscious of his bald head. Speaker kept lifting Lewis' cap to show the bald gleam of it to the crowd during a Fenway batting practice. Lewis said, "You do that again and I'll kill you."

Speaker did it again. Lewis threw a bat at him—and not just casually—hitting Speaker in the shins with such force that he had to be carried from the field.

But the team also had Carrigan, who could hit with his fists as much as with his bat. They won two straight pennants, finished second in 1917, won the pennant again in the war-shortened season of 1918 and took the World Series from the Cubs—a series memorable for a players' strike for a bigger cut of the gate receipts. It held up the start of the fifth game for more than an hour.

Between all that, several things had developed. The Federal League—first intruder, to be followed in successive generations by the Mexican League and the Continental League—began its raiding. Speaker was kept with the Red Sox in 1914 by a salary increase to $18,000. When the Feds collapsed, owner Lannin tried to cut Speaker's salary back to $8,000, but Speaker held out with some reasonable bitterness and was traded on opening day of 1916 to Cleveland.

Carrigan quit after the 1916 season, although only thirty-three, because he recognized the problems pursuant with another development: Lannin sold the club in December of 1916 to a couple of theatrical sharpshooters, Harry Frazee and Hugh Ward.

Frazee is now as much a part of baseball lore as Babe Ruth. A fast talker, he bought in with short money and large notes —later there would be some awesome lawsuits by Lannin—

and there were several scandals concerning him personally. Said to have already made a million dollars in the theater, he made much more than that with the Red Sox in player trades alone, then went on to parlay his holdings in such stage presentations as *No, No Nanette.*

Some say Frazee couldn't adjust to baseball. His other business was strictly a gamble, winning and losing in big chunks. He operated baseball in the same way. Others say he was just typical of one kind of owner in baseball, then and now.

If the modern Yankee dynasty used Kansas City as its major league farm, treadmilling athletes back and forth, then it is probable that the idea first developed with its dealing with Frazee and Boston.

Col. Jacob Ruppert, the very rich brewmeister (much later, by sheer coincidence Ruppert Breweries would buy the Boston Celtics, Ruppert then being owned by Marvin Kratter), and his equally well-heeled partner, who bowed under the weight of being Col. Tillinghast L. Huston, purchased the New York Yankees in 1915.

There was one thing about Frazee, who was New York oriented. Harry the Sharpie could smell money. In 1918, using Ed Barrow as manager (later Barrow went on to the Hall of Fame as the Yankee general manager), Frazee won a pennant. Ruth had been converted to an outfielder in 1918. In 1919 he hit .322 and 29 home runs, four of them grand slams.

What had begun as a few trades now became a steady series. Ruth was traded to the Yankees for $100,000 in 1920 and, secretly, for $350,000 in extra cash, with which the hard-pressed Frazee paid off his old debts to the Lannin interests. Ruppert now had Boston in his clutches and while the fans screamed, Frazee peddled such as Waite Hoyt, Herb Pennock, George Pipgrass and the indefatigable Dugan, who would slowly make his way back to Boston as a scout.

The Yankees won six pennants. Boston sank—scuttled in

what became famous as "the Rape of the Red Sox"—and Frazee sold out to J. A. Robert Quinn, vice-president and business manager of the St. Louis Browns. The year was 1923. Quinn, a good baseball man, certainly wasn't holding the kind of money it took to run a major league team. Instead, he represented the interests of an Indiana glassworks millionaire, Palmer Winslow.

The depression came early for the Red Sox. Dugan and Ruth were swinging in New York. Boston was sinking. Over eleven years the best they could manage was sixth place. Their normal habitat was eighth in an eight-team league. The treadmill to New York continued out of sheer necessity with twilight league games outdrawing the Red Sox while such pitchers as Charlie Ruffing and local-boy Danny MacFayden were sold to the Yanks.

By 1933, the money was gone, "angel" Winslow was dead and Bob Quinn owed $350,000 to Winslow's widow. He did the only thing he could do, selling out to Tom Yawkey, on February 25, 1933.

The resurgence of the Red Sox began, culminating in the 1967 impossible dream.

A brief history, this chapter. But in its own way an important one. The Red Sox are baseball, have been baseball since the beginning of the American League. Good times and bad. Like Massachusetts politics, it always has been fascinating.

3.

The Sportsman

TOM YAWKEY could have been the most controversial man in the history of baseball. That he is not is a direct result of his own clever skill in using the men around him—despite some ineptitudes in the past—and the fact that basically Yawkey is not just a rich man with a plaything. He loves and has been frustrated by baseball, and if there were tears in his eyes when he finally lifted the pennant paper cup of "trembling" with Dick Williams it was because at last—for the very first time in 34 years—he had been given the thrill he always sought; that purest of thrills, a victory which seemed impossible.

There had been one other pennant, of course. That was 1946. If the Red Sox hadn't won that year then it would have been the greatest scandal in the history of the game. They were so filled with talent that they ran away and hid from the rest of the league. By July, it was obvious that they couldn't possibly blow it; although down the stretch they went into such a tailspin that Yawkey ferried the victory champagne from town to town before the pennant was finally clinched in Cleveland on September 13. The victory party naturally wasn't the big story of the day. Ted Williams made certain of that by not showing up for it.

But it was a pennant, even though the World Series against the Cardinals was a seven-game disaster.

From there it was downhill again. Two close shots at it, blowing the first American League playoff game in history in 1948 to Cleveland (while the cross-town Braves were winning the National League), losing the 1949 pennant to the Yankees in the final game of the season.

Maybe Yawkey lost heart after that. There are so many conflicting stories that it is impossible to judge what exactly transpired in Yawkey's front office. Most probably, the intriguers of the sport jammed him up. Joe McCarthy quit suddenly in 1950—smack in mid-season—and Steve O'Neill took over, a nice enough man, whom rookies said it was a pleasure to play for.

O'Neill lasted a season and a half—or, more properly, a half season as McCarthy's replacement and then one full year on his own. Then along came Lou, "dynamic young Lou Boudreau" as he was hopefully called. Boudreau lasted from 1952 to 1954. He introduced "the Youth Movement," which was a costly farce, and disappeared into the wings as Michael F. "Pinky" Higgins came up from the Louisville farm team. Higgins lasted three and one-half seasons—departing suddenly after an argument—and Billy Jurges took over. Jurges won his first five games in a Fourth of July weekend sweep at Yankee Stadium. He was being boohed one week later. He lasted until the middle of 1960 and then Higgins came back, managing in 1961-62 and moving up as general manager when Johnny Pesky took over in 1963. Pesky almost made it through 1964, but was replaced in September by Billy Herman and Herman almost made it for two years but was replaced in late September, 1966, when Dick Williams was appointed.

Put all of that together, coupling it with the other moves which were made about general managers—Eddie Collins to Joe Cronin to Bucky Harris to Higgins to, finally, O'Connell

—and it is very obvious that Yawkey shares as much blame for failure to win a pennant as the worst drunken pitcher in the team's history. (This is a title which remains vacant, it being generally conceded that there were so many strong candidates for the title that it would be unfair to single out one above another.)

Using basic logic, then, it is possible to blame Yawkey. Carrying it one step further, it is also possible to praise him as well. Because they wouldn't have won the pennant in 1967 if he had also not finally begun making the right moves again.

Hence, we have a controversial chapter in this story of the Impossible Dream. Who is Yawkey? What was Yawkey? Exactly what is his total role in baseball?

For myself, I make him a pretty interesting man who has had his own ups and downs. Basically an extraordinarily decent man, he was far too charitable with people who used charity for their own unique purposes. Wildly frustrated, he went through periods where companions over a "jar of the crature," as Thomas Mitchell used to call it in his best Irish idiom, made more sense than strong kids who could hit a long ball and skilled businessmen who could horse-trade for strong kids.

It has never been said before—and one wonders why—but baseball's schemers made Yawkey a sucker. They plucked him of millions, used him as they saw fit and couldn't have cared less that he is one of the last true sportsmen.

Yawkey paved the way for the National League's expansion to the West Coast by first buying the San Francisco franchise for his minor league system and then giving it to his friend, confidant and carefree companion, Horace Stoneham, when Horace needed it to move the Giants from New York as part of the deal with Walter O'Malley.

Yawkey—the kid who once played pepper with Ty Cobb on the lawn of the Detroit mansion where he grew up—sacrificed championships because he was too fond of such as his pet, Ted Williams, and Michael "Pinky" Higgins who presided over their mirthless, yet mirthful demise into a country club.

Owners have been known to enjoy managers and general managers who will share late nights, old stories and good whiskey (which is one reason why Horace Stoneham finally discharged the teetotaling Alvin Dark) and during this period of his gregariousness Yawkey enjoyed both Stoneham and his own general managers.

Yawkey, perhaps unwittingly (but this seems doubtful), also formed the axis which controlled the American League's business affairs as the puppet of first Clark and then Cal Griffith (Washington and Minnesota) and the Detroit Tigers. All of this may have come about because Joe Cronin, his first manager, later his general manager, and still later his appointed American League Commissioner, was a Griffith in-law.

With the exception of occasional forays into the press room in which he scolded writers for some offense (once even threatening to move the Red Sox if they continued to write how poor they were at even trying, let alone how poorly they were playing), Yawkey was seldom seen by the public. He dried up publicly sometime after the 1949 disaster and for years the only photo which could be used in newspapers was the standard full-faced, flush-of-mid-age portrait of a fairly plump man with nicely warm eyes.

Billy Sullivan, the highly controversial president of the Boston Patriots in the American Football League (and former press agent for the Boston Braves) said recently during a period of personal travail:

"My people say I should be like Yawkey. He never made any statements. He let the others talk for him and then he never got in any trouble. Every time I say something I'm in it up to my neck and maybe Yawkey was right at that."

Right or wrong, Yawkey was—at least to the public—un-

Tom Yawkey and Dick O'Connell (standing) watch Manager Dick Williams indicate that the contract he is signing after the 1967 World Series runs for three years.

seen and unheard, a situation which remained constant for nearly 20 years. Shocked they well might have been when he finally emerged. The rotund, robust, two-fisted Yawkey, who was known around baseball's private parts, appeared again on the scene four years ago as a thin, almost emaciated man; a man so unknown that he could walk through his own grandstand without a fan recognizing him. He looked so bad, so really old and ill, that one rumor had him dying of cancer. This was entirely untrue. A lifetime of business tensions and baseball frustrations had contributed to a serious case of diabetes. The old days of Yawkey and his swashbuckling friend Stoneham were over. The suites in such watering stops as the Ritz Carlton in Boston and the Hotel Pierre in New York no longer echoed through late nights.

Now, the true Yawkey was coming out again—and if earlier judgments in this writing have seemed harsh, then it is only equitable to point out that one of the few possible saving graces of baseball in the future can be the true man, Yawkey, the man who saluted Dick Williams: "I haven't taken a drink in four years, but this time I will. Here's to you, Dick."

Whatever he had been, Yawkey was always at the core an enormously decent and humane individual, a man utterly disinterested in the power of his money and concerned for the goodness of man. In his wilder days he had committed the error of mistaking some of his companions, permitting his charity to be vastly misused. And he was charitable: old retainers kept on to provide a retirement home on a major league payroll; carrying sick kids like Gary Geiger because he didn't want them to be without funds or without at least a fighting shot at keeping their pride and their dreams; helping Jimmy Piersall when he was amidst the shattered, nervous wreckage of his young talent; taking over the Jimmy Fund when the Braves moved out of town and contributing millions toward its development as the finest cancer hospital

The end of the country club and the beginning of a pennant team came when grimacing Yawkey listened as O'Connell announced Herman was fired.

Billy Jurges, shown here as a fighting Cubs shortstop, tried hard as manager of the Red Sox Country Club but didn't last long.

for children in the world; doing even such things as this next, one more small story which sums him up:

A Veterans Fund game was scheduled to be played at Fenway Park between the Giants and the Red Sox. Rain canceled it and the expense of team transportation during the next open date was such that it appeared New England's permanently hospitalized veterans would lose approximately $100,000 from the gate receipts (all of which Yawkey was donating with no skim from the top). Yawkey privately, without ever having it known, paid full transportation and other cash payments to athletes and the Giants to put the event on again.

A small thing? Perhaps. But a better indication of the man: the man within. A strange man, involved, filled with feeling, filled with frustration, filled with years of disappointment, dreaming what looked at his age to be an absolutely impossible dream.

We all have our failures. Yawkey's was even larger—and his triumph of 1967 therefore even greater.

To tell of 1967, one must also tell all the background that went into it—the wide panorama of the sport and of the Red Sox, to find this one understanding of the characters, strong, weak, misunderstanding and misunderstood, who finally composed it all in the little toy dream of a world which is baseball played for money in the smallest, but prettiest ball park in the United States.

It began when Yawkey was born. He is often referred to as an "orphan," which is not quite true in the sense which we accept "orphan" to mean. Ruth, by example, was an "orphan," but really not a child without living parents. Incorrigible, he was dispatched to an orphan asylum at the age of seven by a mother and father whose interests appeared to lie more in the recreation of bars than the rearing of children.

Yawkey was orphaned by the death of his mother, and was adopted by his uncle, Bill Yawkey, a millionaire who owned the Detroit Tigers, hence an early introduction to baseball and the chance to play catch with the "ruthless" Cobb in the quiet surroundings of Uncle Bill's showplace mansion.

Young T.A. (for Thomas Austin) was reared to take over his uncle's vast industrial empire (it began with lumber and soared from that into areas which no one is certain of to this day; a private combine, run within the confines of Yawkey's staff in such a manner that if he had not been in baseball he might well have been considered another Howard Hughes, a sometime neighbor of his in the Ritz Carlton Hotel in Boston).

But he also had the bug for baseball, a viral infection which found him such a hero-worshiper that it wasn't until the years directly preceding the 1967 pennant that he discovered there was more hustle in the back rooms than on the field of the grand old game; grand old shell game.

Uncle Bill Yawkey dispatched young T.A. east to Episcopal Academy in New York City, a school whose most distinguished public-print graduate was Eddie Collins, idol of every kid in the school and a man who anchored Connie Mack's $100,000 infield at second base and was, in the course of a varied career, one of the few untainted players on the Black Sox team of 1919. This adoration of Collins—a man who would become most controversial in the Red Sox years which followed—carried over from the baseball team at Episcopal Academy to Yale where T.A. graduated from Sheffield Scientific School while fighting hardest to play second base on the Yale varsity. This effort was not Yawkey's greatest accomplishment. He played enough to keep warm, but not enough to be established in Eli annuals as anything more than a frustrated infielder.

Between the period of graduation and Yawkey's achievement at the age of thirty, Collins had drifted back to the Athletics where he was a coach and was presumably being prepared to take over as manager, when and if Mack ever retired.

But now, in 1933, Yawkey was becoming director of his

own fate. Under the terms of his inheritance from Uncle Bill Yawkey he received all his millions on his thirtieth birthday, February 21, 1933. He had already been shopping to buy a club. Lumber, mines, money—what did it matter if you could be in baseball?

Collins had already been eyeing a deal. Meeting Quinn in midwinter, he negotiated for Yawkey and on February 25, 1933, Quinn presented the new owner to the Boston press.

Ah, 'twas a grand day for the Irish.

Quinn was getting rid of a loser for something over a million dollars. (Which when the bills were paid got him just about even. He showed the good sense of turning down a job with Yawkey, privately saying he just wanted to get as far away from baseball as possible; or at least from Fenway Park.)

Collins was getting a shot at being a general manager at last (imagine if he had stayed as Mack's coach and heir apparent. He would have still been waiting).

Yawkey was getting a baseball team at last.

And what a team it was. The manager was a black-haired Irisher named Marty McManus, who had taken over from John "Shono" Collins, no relation to Eddie Collins, but another who had distinguished himself by being one of the few honest men on the Black Sox. "Shono" quit after watching a completely horrible doubleheader loss to the Indians in mid-1932. McManus was signed up—as later Billy Jurges would be signed—overnight.

"What have you always wanted to be?" McManus was asked by Quinn's traveling secretary. "A manager," said McManus. And a manager he was, throughout '32 and throughout '33 as well, while Yawkey and E. Collins, G.M., began making plans to buy a pennant.

In 1933, the team was a complete loser, but at least Yawkey was being ushered into the big league with laughs. It was all he had . . . characters.

But Collins was beginning to make some deals, backed by untapped millions, and for the 1934 season he had at least some direction and some ideas. One idea was that Stanley "Bucky" Harris would not be the field manager of the Red Sox. (Mr. Harris will be remembered for being mentioned earlier in this chapter as a general manager of the Red Sox during their demise in the decade of the 1950s).

This was one of the few times the highly controversial Collins was overruled by Yawkey. Yawkey knew Harris (about to be dismissed as the manager at Detroit); had indeed known him since Bucky was the original big league "Boy Wonder" with the pennant-winning Senators of 1924. Harris was well-married socially and politically. (To this day his is the only marriage by a baseball player attended by a President of the United States, Calvin Coolidge, and on his honeymoon he was entertained by King George V.) Further, Harris' wife and Yawkey's first wife were close friends.

Collins couldn't have everything, so he took Harris for the 1934 season. Collins also began a series of deals with his old faithful, Connie Mack, in the first of which Yawkey paid nearly a quarter of a million dollars for Lefty Grove, Rube Walberg, and second baseman Max Bishop. Yawkey also paid $750,000 to repair Fenway Park.

In return, Harris—despite front office intrigues, which established the pattern for the future—managed to move Boston up to fourth place in 1934, the first time the team had been in the first division in sixteen years.

Yawkey, in turn, made the first of what might be called his mistakes of friendship. Too gregarious, too much still of a hero-worshiper, he became closely attached to Grove, the great pitcher whose personality could at best not be called pleasing.

The charitable thing is to say that all professional players are thoroughbreds and therefore high-strung. Right? Yep.

This is sports. You go out and get high-strung and they'll either lock you up or you'll get fired. In sports they make allowances for it.

Grove was one of the first of the modern-day pitchers for whom many allowances had to be made. He introduced Yawkey into the world of the legends—which in turn may be why Yawkey made it so easy for Ted Williams and Yastrzemski and others at a later date.

For Grove was really a man of temper. Instinctively, he had the poise and the charm and the timing to handle owners; even such owners as Mack, who was one of the few who permitted Lefty to call him Connie. (Mack in turn called him "Bob," Yawkey called him "Mose" and the public knew him as "Lefty").

When Grove flipped it was a beauty. A wrecked dressing room; a door broken apart; every light in the tunnel leading to the dressing room shattered. (I wonder if that scene seems familiar to the modern Red Sox?) But he was also wise enough to carefully shatter everything with his right hand. The left hand was payday.

Yawkey was not being initiated in only this way. Wes Ferrell flipped so badly one day that he ground his wristwatch under his foot. (Later, in 1936, he was to become the first of the free spirits, a true expressionist, thumbing his nose at the fans, a gesture on which Ted Williams would often improve at a later date.) The gags and the gagsters ranged from putting possums into the rooms of clubhouse boys to planting stink bombs in Yawkey's drawing room. Ha, ha. So many funnies that in '34 Harris was also equipped with a large bankroll to bail out the drunks.

Harris had other managerial problems as well. The Red Sox have always been famous for palace plots. Their history has more coups d'état than Vietnam. Harris didn't figure to last. G.M. Collins had him sharp-shot out of the picture by the September mark (always a witching time for the Sox) and even though the Sox were in fourth place Harris was on his way.

That put Collins in sole command again. His reign would continue until Joe Cronin replaced him in 1948. For all those years in between, Cronin—who would be the next Red Sox field manager—sweated it out; eating his heart out sometimes at Collins' second-guessing, but hiding it under an ever-hardening shell.

This was unfortunate. Cronin, in the beginning, was the ideal dream of what baseball is all about. A kid who fought his way up from the sandlots of San Francisco, he was a superb shortstop, the youngest manager ever to win a pennant (twenty-seven with the Senators in 1933). He married Mildred Robertson, a niece of Mrs. Clark Griffith, wife of the owner of the Senators (it was obviously love and therefore men in baseball did not originally hold the relationship to Griffith against him). He became successively the manager of the Red Sox, then general manager, and the Yawkey-Griffith axis steered him to the office of President of the American League. His own talents earned him election to the Hall of Fame in 1956 and when in 1966-67 it came time to vote for the new Commissioner of Baseball it figured Cronin would be the logical choice. Sandlot rags to riches. Ford Frick would pass his rubber stamp into stronger hands. Hurrah for the American Dream.

Instead, Cronin could not muster the necessary votes. The owners voted the Eckert ticket—an event comparable to Henry Wallace winning the Presidency—and something happened in all of that which once again involves Yawkey.

It was Yawkey who brought Cronin to the Red Sox, with the guile of Collins (if $250,000 can be considered guile). It was Yawkey who moved Cronin along. Yet, according to an authoritative, if angry, source—baseball writer and veteran Clif Keane—it was Yawkey who sold Cronin out for the job of Commissioner of Baseball. Keane, insisting that his source was accurate and finally admitting it was Gene Autry of the Angels, states most emphatically:

"Yawkey did the job on Cronin. Autry told me the story time and time again. The owners figured T.A. was going to go for Cronin. Instead, Yawkey sat there and did such a job on Cronin that it eliminated him for good. Autry told me he was never so shocked at anything in all his life. Never heard such stories. And he has given me the same facts six different times—always the same way, so I have to believe it is true."

It is true. It will never be corroborated. Baseball is that kind of a game. But whatever happened, Yawkey gave and Yawkey took away. But that was thirty-one years after he first brought Cronin to the Red Sox.

Any guy has a right to change his mind?

Right?

Right.

4.

The League President

THE cast of characters grows longer now. The transition seems to cover a wider gamut than just the story of the 1967 Red Sox who went from the country club life to success in the impossible dream.

But each man in his own fashion was still there in the windup. Yawkey the owner. Cronin, now the American League President. Dugan, the comrade of Ruth, and others who will be named as the modern Red Sox developed.

"It's the strangest damn team in the history of baseball," a man said, watching them in the World Series. "The Gas House Gang, the old Dodgers, the Yanks, whatever. The Red Sox have had more characters, more great players, more drunks and more guys in the Hall of Fame than anyone I can think of. The only thing is, why didn't they win more often?"

Cronin had his own answers for that, but he learned long ago to cease voicing his opinions. He was in trouble often enough in the early days. Outspoken. Tough. Baseball has the Pavlovian theory, you know. They don't ring the bell. But slap the guy down often enough and he reacts. The mouth shuts. The heart is still the same, however.

Joe Cronin, let it be said here, has a big heart. So does Tom

Yawkey. It got both of them in trouble. But they both still have it. So if they didn't achieve everything, at least they didn't completely fail either.

Cronin came to the Red Sox in 1935 as playing manager. If he made any errors at shortstop it was understandable. He was often afraid to leave the dugout. His cast of characters would immediately get into trouble, ranging from Wes Ferrell walking off the mound (Cronin hit him with a $1,000 fine) to fistfights in the dugout (Werber and Dahlgren). If Harris needed a bankroll for drunks, then Cronin needed an even bigger one. Not only that, but he had more "clubhouse lawyers" and there was constant talk of dissension on the team and of terrible working conditions. This seems about as farfetched as it can get when one considers the money Yawkey paid and the even temperament of the manager. But it has ever been so at Boston. Or was until 1967.

In addition to which, Cronin didn't have any pitching to speak of. Yawkey—determined to pull a Frazee in reverse and buy a pennant—was still out shopping with his aide, Collins, who knew his way around the markets. The two men sought for a long time to get Jimmy Foxx from the Athletics and when the 1935 league meetings rolled around they completed a deal with Mack for $150,000, most of which went for Foxx.

Mack—waving his program to give the signs; sitting there in the high old collar; wearing the straw hat—is the public relations dream of baseball. He was always remembered by the fans as "Grand Old Connie" from the "Grand Old Game."

"Grand Old Connie" didn't survive in the big leagues all those seasons because he was a Sunday school teacher. Beneath the straw hat lurked a brain of cold, hard, practical steel. He had a bead on Yawkey's bankroll through the sharp eyes of his old student, Collins, and he sold off players who

Cronin was a great Hall of Famer, but he had some wild players on his Red Sox teams.

Joe Cronin singles against Yanks in great days as Sox playing manager.

had helped win three pennants with as much care as Frazee completed the Rape of the Red Sox in the Twenties.

Ty Cobb loved to tell stories in his seventies. Angry stories. True ones. Cobb and Rogers Hornsby were not exactly lovable men. The Black Sox scandal of 1919 was not exactly in the best interests of the "grand old shell game" and the scandal reached much, much deeper than that. Everyone knew that there was much more to it and the appointment of another baseball "legend," Judge Kenesaw Mountain Landis, as Baseball Commissioner was not in the interest of cleaning up the mess publicly. Landis' job was to expose only those who must be exposed and sweep the rest under the rug, sections of which, as mentioned earlier, Bill Veeck—one of baseball's more charming rogues—found years later behind an old table in Chicago's Comiskey Park.

Along the way, there was some information which worked to the detriment of Cobb (Detroit manager) and Hornsby (Cleveland manager). Landis dumped them both. Cobb—the vision comes back so strongly of him sitting in his robe time and again, telling me the story—went home to Royston, Georgia, and wired Landis.

"I told him: 'Nobody drives Old Ty out of this game. Either I play or I talk. You decide.'

"Shortly after that, Mack stopped by my house. 'How much, Mr. Cobb?' says he.

" '$100,000, Mr. Mack,' says I.

" 'I knew I shouldn't have stopped in Georgia,' says Mack. 'Sign here, Mr. Cobb.'

"They used old Connie to buy me off. It figured they would. Connie was involved with them all from the start; the guys like Somers who owned four different teams from Chicago to Boston and all the rest. He was clean. They knew they could depend on him to keep his mouth shut. He paid me and I played for the Athletics for two more years just to prove to them that they couldn't drive Old Ty out of baseball."

Cronin meets with Babe Ruth while Cronin was boy wonder manager at Washington.

Cronin shakes with Cards manager Eddie Dyer in first World Series between teams in 1946.

Cobb invested it in something called Coca-Cola. Mack was paid the majority of the salary on the side by all the owners.

But now it was a decade and more later and he was dealing in front. Money glowed from Yawkey's big bankroll. The players shuttled up from the Athletics. Foxx, the most glamorous hitter since Ruth—and a decent, lovable man of little education and little native erudition—was one more purchase which supposedly spelled pennant.

Except you don't win pennants without pitchers. Cronin had nothing. Grove was becoming more pliable, actually changing into a nice personality as he staggered toward his greatest desire, 300 wins, in the twilight of a superb career. Wes Ferrell was just totally unpredictable. Johnny Marcum, who came along from the A's with Foxx, started the 1936 season by having his tonsils out, items which he carried around in a jug and proudly displayed as the largest, perhaps, ever seen in medical history. Marcum, it might be said, was slow to respond. Like the day a fan asked him if he had been to church.

"Sure," said Marcum.

"Which church?" asked the fan.

"Name me a couple," Marcum said.

The '36 Sox also had a good outfielder, Heinie Manush. But his major fame, to those of us old enough to remember trains and sleepers, came from the movies. The star, trying to sleep over the clacking wheels, kept repeating: "Heinie Manush . . . Heinie Manush."

Try it sometime. Nightmares.

And that's what the Red Sox were to Cronin and to a Yawkey who was getting more and more angry. The bankroll bought nothing. 1935-36-37. Zeros. Grief and dissension among some of the egos. Intrigues in the front office.

They tried to develop something else. The Yankees and the Cardinals—two teams which consistently reappear intertwined in the fate of the Red Sox—were doing well with farm systems.

"Okay," said Yawkey. "We'll try to build our own talent." He created a farm system and appointed a former umpire, Billy Evans, to head the minor league chain and meanwhile sat and fidgeted while Cronin and his hitters (among whom was third baseman Mike Higgins, who one day would be manager and general manager) frittered away T.A.'s impossible dream of a world champion.

It also, coincidentally, was the wrong time to snap the rubber band on the bankroll. For $25,000 there was a kid named Joe DiMaggio available. It was said he might have a bad knee. Yawkey took no chances. The verdict was "No." It leads one to wonder about fate and the matter of timing. Still, all was not wasted. The loss of DiMaggio ultimately led to the signing of Williams.

Williams. A chapter unto himself.

A chapter? It should be a book. Except that he will never permit it to be written.

But in all of this there was still what became the 1967 Red Sox. Williams, Ted and Dick, would have their part. Cronin would have his. Bobby Doerr, whose ability first led Collins west to look at talent and the discovery of Williams, would be the best coach on the 1967 Red Sox. DiMaggio? Well, he was long since gone. But his brother, Dom, would still be around, a rich man now and waiting in the wings to buy the Red Sox if and when Tom Yawkey retired, frustrated that the dream could never be; the dream that became reality in 1967, the Year of the Yaz.

5.

Williams the First

HE was the strangest of them all. To this very moment, not even those who played beside him have any understanding of who or what he is; of what he dreamed, of where he aimed; of where he achieved and where he failed.

Cobb privately thought he was the worst team player in the history of the game, but publicly admitted that he was also the greatest hitter he had ever seen.

Cronin privately thought him something less than one of the finest athletes the game ever produced—publicly saying the right words, of course—but ultimately setting the record straight for all time when he cast his vote for Stan Musial as the Player of the Decade in the *Sporting News* poll of 1955.

Joe DiMaggio privately thought him a mixed-up guy who blew his real chance at greatness with a poor sense of public relations; yet his teammate, Dom DiMaggio, so admired him he didn't even mind it when he sometimes had to play both his own center field position and a portion of left field.

And Eddie Collins and Tom Yawkey loved him. No holds barred. Win, lose, draw, trauma, dramatic home runs or tossed bats and spitting episodes.

He was, simply, Ted Williams, which is at one and the

same time the least and the most far-ranging description of him.

It is interesting that despite the possibility of almost $100, 000 in guaranteed royalties, neither Williams nor DiMaggio will ever permit their full stories to be told. Yet "the Kid" and "the Yankee Clipper" were baseball for nearly twenty seasons, in ten of these matching one legend against the other for Most Valuable Player Awards, batting championships and the American League pennant.

Perhaps this refusal to undergo the autobiographical surgery of another writer's pen is because each has had a personal life which could not be overlooked; a personal life, that is to say, which is not any better or any worse than those of many men. But they were public symbols. The legends. Caught up in it. And if now, in their silent seasons, all the stories were told, then indeed it might be the private people who surrounded them, wives, children, friends, who would suffer the greater hurt.

So, definitely, neither will ever tell all. Yet, in writing of the Red Sox, even to this year of the impossible dream, the story would be incomplete without either one.

Each could have been a member of the Red Sox. Yawkey, trying to buy his pennant, passed up the chance at DiMaggio for $25,000 from the Pacific Coast League, because scouting reports said he had a chronically bad knee.

Collins, scouting Bobby Doerr and someone long since forgotten, named George Myatt, saw Williams on the only trip he ever took to California. He made an offer to San Diego Padres' owner Bill Lane on the spot, but Lane—eminently honest—turned it down. Williams was just a wild pitcher, seventeen years old. "But," Lane said, "I'll tell you what. I will give you a chance to match the best offer if he ever develops."

The legend is that Collins saw Williams hit two long home runs the first time he saw him. But that's just another legend.

Actually, Collins saw mainly just the potential and always said later on, "Anyone could have done it. I was just lucky that I was there."

Oddly, it was Casey Stengel who started the bidding. Stengel had been paid not to manage Brooklyn in 1937 and spent the season watching his California investments and the Pacific Coast League. He put in a bid for Williams for the Boston Braves, whom he would manage in 1938.

Baseball—to steal a title from Garagiola—is a funny game and nothing could be more unusual than the total twists which are involved here. Stengel came back to Boston to the humpty-dumpty Braves in 1938 and in 1943—after securely holding seventh place for four straight seasons—was struck by a cab one stormy night, suffering a broken leg. Columnist Dave Egan, who was to play a major role in Williams' life as well, coined the epitaph of Stengel of the Braves which will always be remembered: "The cab driver who struck down Casey Stengel," he said, "deserves the award as the man who has done the most for Boston baseball this year."

Stengel went on to the Yankees and consistently beat the Red Sox for the pennant, while at the same time carrying on a sub-rosa feud with DiMaggio. Williams settled in Boston to become columnist Egan's favorite target—skewered on a typewriter which first named him "the Splendid Splinter" (Bill Cunningham tabbed Williams "the Kid"). Cronin, the shortstop-manager of Williams' first Red Sox club, became Commissioner of the American League and reportedly had a shot at Commissioner of Baseball on Ford Frick's retirement until Yawkey shot him down in an executive meeting of the owners. Doerr came back to coach the pennant-winning Sox of this year and Ted Williams—vice-president of the team—went fishing up north and never even bothered to come to a World Series game.

That's getting ahead of all the story, sure. But beautiful, isn't it? Only in baseball. Only, particularly, in Boston and, most surely, only with Ted Williams. He could get in trouble giving a gift to the United Fund.

And quite possibly he is the only one you'll ever meet who would enjoy getting into that kind of trouble. It followed him wherever he went—from the moment Collins first saw him to the postmortems on this year's World Series when everyone had to come up with a reason why Ted wasn't there.

In point of truth, he wasn't there because he didn't feel wanted. Williams the First never did get along with Williams the Second. A quick flash of words at spring training. Two egos clashing. Then, in September, Dick Williams sent Frank Malzone off to scout the Cardinals.

Now it was clear forever. There was a new Williams in charge in Boston—and there wasn't room for two. "Ted never impressed me as a player," Dick Williams said.

The story will get around that Ted really didn't show up because he didn't want to hog the spotlight. But it's a cover-up and in one way it's a shame that he wasn't there and in another a credit to the cockiness of Dick Williams that he was strong enough to keep him away.

It wasn't always so. A succession of Red Sox managers would attest to that. Yawkey didn't want to buy Williams in 1938 when Collins insisted on it. Having fallen on his financial face in the attempt to buy a pennant he now wanted to put money into the farm system. But Collins insisted and whatever Eddie finally wanted he always got from Yawkey. Besides, Collins was smart in the clutch. He knew the most convincing argument of all—did Yawkey want to go down in baseball history as the owner who let both Joe DiMaggio and Ted Williams get away?

Williams, gangling, all arms and legs and false cockiness, came to spring training at Sarasota. Proud—too proud—and too cocky and not understanding the rules which required at least one more year of seasoning. Stepping into trouble from the start with Cronin and with the writers. But stepping, somehow, into the heart of Yawkey at the same time. Of them all, it was Williams who reached the touchstone. He was Yawkey's man from start to finish and always will be.

There are others who consider him something less. His full measure lies somewhere in between, this man of fascination, profane to the point he could make you want to puke; gentle to the point he could make you want to cry to see him with a sick child; defiant, furiously—and stupidly—defiant against the Boudreau shift; gallant—defiantly gallant—as he demanded of the Marine Corps that he be sent to combat during the Korean conflict.

There are flashing personal images of Williams:

The blue-black Panther jet, trailing smoke, light white, red flames licking at it, coming down across the deck toward Kimpo field in Korea, the pilot holding it up almost with his hands; the people on the ground watching, waiting for it to go up with the quick flame like you strike a match and man and plane are gone. But instead the pilot lugs it into the field now, all a black smudge of smoke while two taxiing jets suddenly dart out of the way and another cuts in a burner and moves up, up out of the way fast.

The F-9 scuttles into the strip, sludging, twisting, ripping itself to scrap and huddling to a stop, and the last glimpse is the pilot, a huge man, getting out fast through the smoke as the fire engines come up.

A Ranger group, back in from a canceled raid, is stripping chutes and equipment by a C-47 and someone says: "Whee . . . what a lucky sonofabitch that guy is." Someone else says: "Crazy. Don't they give them pilots parachutes?"

Later, someone else says: "Hey, do you know who was in that plane today? Ted Williams, that's who. Ted Williams. What the hell is he doing in Korea?" And later still he is seen sitting around the club with his squadron, the long arms with the seemingly delicate hands describing arcs and swoops and whatever those guys do up there at 30,000; head back, laugh-

Ted Williams in his prime, slashing a long home run.

Williams also in his prime as he raged and threw bat which hit Cronin's housekeeper on head.

The last of the .406 hitters, Williams had superb hitting style.

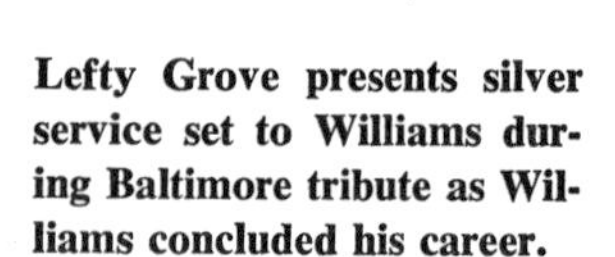

Lefty Grove presents silver service set to Williams during Baltimore tribute as Williams concluded his career.

ing, more relaxed and comfortable than he has ever been seen before or since.

There is the image another fighter pilot in WW II has of Williams during one Christmas leave at the Pre-Flight School at Chapel Hill. Williams had nowhere to go. Another kid had a home in Boston. Williams reached into his kick for the fare. "G'wan, Bush," he said. "G'wan. I'll stand your duty. Christmas doesn't mean nothin' to me."

If one is to conclude the proud history of a man who was a brilliant warrior in the last playground of the individualist

Williams gags with Pumpsie Green as the latter became the first Negro to play for the Red Sox in 1959.

—fighters at 30,000 feet—then it must also be the Williams who quietly dug into pocket again to pay for the initial burdens and future scholarships of the family of another recalled Reservist who was killed in Korea.

That was one side; the flip side of the Kid, a kid who also when he was very young was known to give his lunch money to others in San Diego. That was how he was trained by his mother, a devout and gentle lady, defamed (Ted thought) by a misunderstanding press during his early days as an athlete.

It may be this relationship which leads one more truly to the real Williams. But the course of discovering the real Williams is almost obscured by the legend, whether it be the legend of the baseball player, the Marine or just that of the temperamental Kid.

If the Marines and his real manhood—ranging even now to his personally sought isolation and his kinship with tarpon, salmon and the pursuit of game with few friends—is one side, the flip side; then the public side of his record is equally enchanting.

Williams the First strode to stage center in baseball and stayed there from the start. The legend has been distorted. This is only one small attempt to put the record completely straight, since the Kid will never even try; since the aging man with the middle-age paunch will just automatically seek and permit controversy to always swirl around him; controversy to the point that finally, in 1967, even his deepest admirer, Yawkey, was not surprised when he failed to show up for the Series. Privately, even Yawkey would finally admit: "Who knows? Who ever did understand him? You just take him like you find him. I've just given up, completely."

Williams' greatest rival, Joe DiMaggio, was coming back into baseball, signing on with Charlie Finley as the Athletics moved even farther west, seeking gold in Oakland. Williams was moving farther north and out of it entirely.

Gone fishin', Jack. Just gone fishin' up north. All the stories in the world by well-intended friends: "Ted really cared; Ted watched each game on TV" are so much bushwa, fed to exceptionally gifted sportswriters of integrity and using their reputations and ability as a cover-up. The fact is T.W. frankly couldn't have cared less. Not when it's time to go fishin', man. Not when he felt unwanted. He was very happy to say, "The hell with them."

In Boston, Williams the Second—deftly experienced in the jungle of the major leagues—was happy to respond in kind.

Yet, if Williams did not share in the impossible dream, it would not really have been possible without him. For he kept the interest alive in baseball through the dead days. The last of the .400 hitters (.406 to be exact) always had a sixth sense about the fellow cartoonists call Joe Phan.

It might have been anything—from giving the unforgivable sign (or at least unforgivable until Hollywood decided anything goes), to spitting, to throwing bats, to assaulting his friends, the Knights of the Keyboard.

His favorite expression, if he likes you, is "Bush." His favorites are few. Since this is a pin—Freudian slip—pen and ink portrait, let it be said here that as a sportswriter who did not have to put up with him every day I always respected him. If I had had to put up with him every day, then that might have been another matter—easily resolved, one would think, by direct confrontation, the one tactic Williams respected best.

All of this, however, diverts from the central fact—the chronicle of the man, both public and private.

The first appearance of Williams is as a fifteen-year-old, gangling pitcher for the "Fighting Bob" American Legion Post in San Diego. His pitching was less impressive than the fact that he hit a ball out of the park and through a store window. A Yankee scout, Bill Essick, watched his progress closely from that point—even making a small bid to Williams' mother, May; but his mother didn't want him leaving home. Instead, she permitted Ted to play for the newly formed San Diego Padres where Bill Lane promised he would not permit Ted to be traded until he was twenty-one and that if he ever was able to sell him to the big leagues he would give May 10 percent of the sale price.

As things developed, it turned out that Collins was finally able to convince Yawkey to buy Williams and as things also developed San Diego owner Lane, while scrupulously honoring his agreement with Collins, refused to give Mrs. Williams her 10 percent.

It seems like a small storm now in light of all that Williams has been through, but in 1938 the story blew up out of all proportion until Collins gave Mrs. Williams $2,500. It is most important because Williams himself felt his mother was given an unnecessarily difficult time in the press—and responded in kind to writers ever after.

Mrs. Williams was always a devoted Salvation Army worker. Williams himself was "dedicated" to the organization as a boy. As the years went on, he became overly protective of his mother and a brother, Danny, who was not as successful. The result was a legend of a Williams who was ashamed of his family and about "Salvation May," facts which could not be further from the truth, but facts which had a strong bearing on all his relations with the press and the public for the remainder of his career.

Of course, Williams always could put his foot in his mouth. That first year, coming up to spring training he was accompanied by Doerr and Babe Herman. After they dodged California floods, they finally arrived ten days late for spring training. It was raining in Florida. Williams' first crack was:

"So this is Florida? Do they always keep it under a foot of water?"

It was the bravado of a young kid and should have been accepted as such, but writers already accustomed to wild stories were looking for another "screwball" to liven spring training. Williams was off and running.

The first-year stories established the legend. Of course he was cocky. Batting against Herb Pennock for cameramen he hit without a cap. Advised to put it on, he grinned: "Is this all it takes to be a big-leaguer? I thought it would be tougher than this."

The kid had style, but he had a lot to learn and his shyness and nervousness rubbed off in crazy statements and crazier stunts as his bat failed against big league pitching; ridiculing Florida first, then aiming at Boston ("If I knew I was going to Boston I'd have taken a scholarship at Southern Cal") and galloping through the outfield, slapping his side and yelling: "Hi-ho, Silver, awa-a-a-y" as he chased (and usually missed) fly balls.

Someone should have reined him in. Eddie Collins could have and through the later years, Collins seemed to provide more care and interest for Williams than anyone else. But in these first days he was just a frightened nineteen-year-old who knew he wasn't making good. He was one of the first shipped to the minors, dispatched to Minneapolis after temperamental jams with Cronin which might have been easily avoided. (It could not be considered Cronin's fault. He had his hands full with some of his team, still.) The big mistake was in not telling Williams when he first signed that he would have to spend at least one year in the high minors. He was crushed when he was sent to Minneapolis in the American Association.

He was a wild kid there, a kid who drove seasoned manager Donie Bush to distraction. The stunts: practicing batting while playing right field, talking back to the fans, his back to the plate with the bases loaded, missing fly balls and refusing to run them out and becoming so bored at one time that he sat down in right field. His base running also left something to be desired. (Bush recalls Williams reaching second on a double and taking a long, long lead while Bush yelled for him to get back. "Take it easy," Williams said. "I got here by myself. And I'll get back.")

Fresh kid or not, he led the league in batting with .366, in homers with 43, in runs scored with 130 and in runs batted in with 142.

His off-field antics were just as bad: tearing up uniforms, ruining a locker room (Cronin with the characters he already had at Fenway must have really relished this information) and finally, climactically, becoming so angry one day that he rammed his fist through a water jug after popping up.

He was lucky the hand was saved. Manager Bush, up to his ears with it, appealed to Collins, requesting Williams' assignment elsewhere, or permission to discipline him by suspension. Collins wired back: WHEN WILLIAMS DOESN'T PUT HIS UNIFORM ON, DON'T YOU BOTHER EITHER.

Collins planned to build a new Yankee dynasty around Williams. When the chance availed itself, they traded the troublesome Ben Chapman to Cleveland, even though he was a .340 hitter. Williams reported to spring training in 1939 to stay—and naturally enough he reported a week late.

Cronin has often been criticized for not being harder on Williams from the start. Still, what else could Cronin do? He had his hands full with others in the clubhouse and on the field and was very well aware that Williams was Collins' and Yawkey's boy. He did the logical thing and put up with it—getting in his final licks in 1955 when he voted for Stan Musial as Player of the Decade instead of Williams. In baseball, everything evens up.

It took a long time. Williams was up to stay, but he was still up to tricks. One wonders still what he ever had in his mind. Stopping off in Atlanta on their way home, Williams, who always idolized Babe Ruth, wanted to hit three home runs in the park as Ruth had once done. Instead, he tripled with the bases loaded first time up, struck out the next time and struck out again with two men on base in the eighth. He threw his bat a pretty far piece in disgust—the first of a bat-throwing series which would later cause him trouble. As he took the field in the eighth, the fans got on him. Teddy screamed right back, following this up by dropping a foul fly he had in his glove, turning slowly and *throwing the ball right over the top of the grandstand.*

Only a Williams could have gotten away with it. The press might have been a little nervous over this kid and Cronin might have been downright distraught, but the Boston fans took to him in a love affair which had frequent separations but never ended in divorce.

There is a legend that Williams would never tip his cap, but this is not so. In those earlier days, playing right field, jabbering with the people in the Fenway grandstand, he was their darling and one can still remember him trotting back out to right field after a big hit and hoisting the cap up high.

Somewhere things went awry for this man. The accusation that he was never a team player and never a winner may seem true on the surface. There is no doubt that he and he alone was responsible for a Red Sox team attitude toward press and public that did neither any good. Nor is there any doubt that he did not inspire his mates. It will always be questionable exactly whose fault it was.

One can blame him for being sulky and "bush" in not attending the World Series of 1967 while friends will claim that he really didn't want to upstage the team and hog the coverage. (This seems unlikely in view of all that transpired with these miracle Red Sox as they faltered to the flag in a four-team giveaway race.) But one can also understand that beneath there is a troubled man of some greatness, whose private deeds were equally as fascinating as his public ones.

From the beginning, Williams would take kids to Revere Beach (years later he became the most indefatigable worker for the Jimmy Fund Hospital and still is); would take the clubhouse boys fishing; would do charitable things, spending as much money as he was making.

He was a master of the niceties of hitting and the unnecessaries of public life. Babe Ruth was fond of using an air rifle to shoot squirrels on golf courses. Williams, a marksman, one-upped the Babe by shooting pigeons at Fenway. When he became bored, he shot out all the lights on the scoreboard, the $400 cost of which Yawkey bore with a smile, while writers raged about the Kid and his temperament.

They hooked him once because on an off day at Yankee Stadium he visited an uncle who was a fireman in Yonkers and returned to say: "That's the life. When I retire I think I'll be a fireman and sit around all day playing checkers."

That crack was all Jimmy Dykes of the White Sox needed. Years later, in the stretch drive for the pennant, Eddie Stanky with these same White Sox would attempt to get Yastrzemski to blow his cool stating "Yaz is a great ballplayer from the neck down," and Yaz would retaliate with one of his greatest series. Dykes, fortified with something even more tangible, outfitted his bench with firehats and a siren, teasing Williams each time he came to bat. Williams was hitting, however, and the technique didn't work any better than that of Stanky in 1967.

By his sophomore year, Williams was an idol, a joke and a controversy. He appeared to enjoy being all three. Cronin moved him to left field. In that first year Cronin had enough grief. Williams consistently practiced his swing in right. Finally, Cronin stopped a game and pantomined at great length instructions which indicated, "Hey, never mind the swinging. You could use some practice fielding."

Another time—trailing Jimmy Foxx by two RBIs in the race which Williams finally won to become the first rookie to lead the A.L. in this department—the Kid popped to short center and loafed in disgust to first. The ball fell for a hit.

Williams should have made it to second. Cronin immediately benched him. Williams, in the next game, showed his humor by racing out a tap to the pitcher and casting to the crowd that huge kiddish grin.

The Red Sox weren't that good a team and Cronin constantly sought something to perk up the gate. He even put Williams in to pitch once again Detroit for the final two innings. Williams survived with only one run scored against him—and that by Mike Higgins, who would later be his manager and as the Red Sox G.M. preside over the disaster of the country club in the early 1960s.

In his sophomore year, Williams was moved to left. He still plagued Cronin. "I had to look over my shoulder to be sure he was there." Williams just had to be himself. He would do many things, including his customary checking of out-of-town scores and home runs with the man behind the wall scoreboard who had ready access to the baseball ticker and—during one mid-inning when he was sure he was not coming to bat—*walking* through the scoreboard, out the back door and across the street to get a plate of ice cream.

Beautiful.

Only in Boston.

A Boston where Williams would so involve and direct his teammates that there was a locker-room sign: No Writers Please; and a Boston where, after his final and most dramatic homer of all, one writer said, "Now that he's gone we'll find out if it was just Williams or whether Boston attracts all the —— in baseball." Until late September of 1967, the same writer was still certain that as a result of the Williams attitude Boston did indeed attract all the —— in baseball.

Yet, there is more to it than that, if one can ever find the touchstone of it all. Williams, in his own way, was as superb as any part of the American Dream. It would never do to have him on the backside of a package of Wheaties. But he was always one of those who somehow kinned backward to the memory of the Mountain Men and the individualists who sought their own far frontier.

He was alternately charming and bitter; alternately capable and inept.

In the history of the game of baseball, he will be marked off with his idol, Ruth, and his once friend, then deadly enemy, Cobb, and with his greatest personal opponents, DiMaggio and Musial.

Of them all, Musial—who would lead the Cardinals to the championship of the world in 1967—stands out as The Man, for in Musial there was sheer, unrestrained goodness, untempered by hard knocks. Among the others, there was always controversy.

Williams vs. DiMaggio is the biggest internal feud of them all, the dominant factor of the 1939–1950 period of baseball when it swung into the money game through the channels of TV and through the demonstrable cashier's checks of owners who caught it on the upswing, staggered through WW II as the Great American Dream and parlayed it past Congress to keep their slave trade the only business in America which cannot be properly controlled.

On the one hand, Williams had to admire Joe DiMaggio. He was so conscious of him and so considerate of his brother, Dom, who played Boston's center field, that during Joe's 1941 hitting streak of 56 straight games, Williams would each day check the scoreboard machine and call over when Dom's brother had achieved another hit.

On the other hand, he had a bitterness. In this same year, 1941, when Williams hit .406—and hit it courageously by not quitting in the final series, but hitting despite a personal ailment—DiMaggio was the Most Valuable Player.

Williams would say privately, "I don't understand some of this. I keep myself in good shape. I don't get in brawls in nightclubs. Hell, it's been known for years that the New York writers protect DiMaggio. When he can't field they don't mention it. When he's in trouble they keep it out of the papers. But he's the big star. I just don't figure what it's all about. What *is* the difference?"

When DiMaggio finally retired, at the age of thirty-six after hitting .263, Williams couldn't resist a public statement: "When I hit .260 I'll retire, too."

And it is a fact that after the 1946 World Series there was a very strong move between the Yankees and the Red Sox to trade Williams even-up for Joe DiMaggio, a deal which will always be denied but which was nearly made.

Cronin, who watched DiMaggio for thirteen years lead the Yankees to ten pennants and nine World Series championships, summed it up: "So what? Even if we traded what do you think would have happened? The Yankees still would have won. They had more depth."

That may be the final answer. The feud of pride is a normal thing in this public world where men make their names with a bat in their hands.

Williams, faulted always for failing to hit in Yankee Stadium, actually had a lifetime .307 average there. "But no one ever remembers that," he will say.

Well, what are they to remember? Did he make the Red Sox? Did he ruin them?

There will never be an answer. Even time cannot solve this issue, nor a thousand hours of discussion with one foot on a bar rail. They were two separate egos, two separate and distinct men, and this chapter is concerned with Williams the First and his contribution, domination and, finally, major influence in the history of this team which finally accomplished the impossible dream under the iron-handed direction of Williams the Second.

All of it was influenced by Williams the First. The last of the .400 hitters, the man who did so many memorable things in All Star games, in regular season, in the Marine Corps, and who so completely failed in the one World Series the Red Sox ever played before 1967.

If this chapter ranges wide, then it is because he was a man of vast proportion, of vast feeling; a man who would give his World Series check in 1946 to a clubhouse boy, Johnny Orlando (and later give him his Cadillac). A man who was terribly harassed by the press for not immediately joining the service in 1941, yet finally had a much more creditable service record than most athletes—and a man who was equally attacked because he was not present for the birth of his only child, a daughter, in 1948.

These, too, are parts of Williams, parts which must be understood.

It is essential that they be understood, because everything about him permeated this team—leading it down to the depths and then shocking them back out of it. They would not have been a highly paid, failing country club except for Williams and an attitude which influenced the front office. They would not have banded together again except for the courage of Dick Williams—and because in his growing years Williams the First would finally take Carl Yastrzemski aside in spring training, 1967, and make a compleat player out of him; a compleat hitter; a compleat man with the press; a compleat leader; a compleat competitor.

Having done that, Williams the First then went off to sulk.

Figures.

Ted Williams' playing record seeming to be such a part of the public domain, something which will always be a complete matter for the public, it is necessary here to digress and tell a few more untold facts about him. This matter, for one, of his "draft dodging" in WW II.

When Williams hit .406 in 1941 he was earning something around $12,000 a year. He was 3-A in the pre-war draft, having declared his mother a dependent. When Yawkey, at the end of 1941, upped his salary to $25,000-plus, Williams added to a trust fund for his mother's protection.

The war began and Williams was made 1-A, but asked for a reclassification and went to spring training. He received a 3-A again and came to spring training in 1942 to answer the grilling questions heroic editors demanded be asked by reporters on the scene. (This is a most compelling commentary on the press, since I know for a fact that one such editor was himself taken off the 1-A list because he was "essential to the morale" of the people. In ensuing wars he has constantly sought to dodge the draft of his sons. Yet, he was one of the strongest in attacking Williams, using a purple-prosed columnist whose own heroics were confined to refusing a drink. Later, this columnist drank himself to death, often accusing the editor of betraying him, his ideals and sundry other persons. A passing scene of little importance in the total comprehension of the climate and times, but still of some value in seeking to understand it all.)

Williams' answer was terse and to the point: "I'm ducking nothing. I wanted to make a few more bucks before I go in, to take care of my mother. When I do go in, it won't be into some physical fitness program."

When he did enlist, it was Marine Aviation, the stories of which have been recounted previously.

In 1948, there was the matter of not being present for the birth of his daughter. Williams was fishing. The baby, now a full-grown woman and a lovely one, was born two weeks prematurely. By the time Williams returned to Boston, he was the subject of much dissent in the purpler press and among the fans. It seems rather odd now. Perhaps other fathers were just getting rid of their repressions. The war was over. Men were home and 1948 was the year of the baby boom.

So, Williams went fishing. Hurrah. Maybe other guys wished they could, too.

No, these highlights are not the important parts of the man, nor of the Red Sox. It is not even important that Williams lost the MVP trophy to DiMaggio in 1947 by one vote, 202-201, because a Boston writer refused even to list him among the top ten. It was a bush-league stunt, admittedly, but it wasn't fatal. Williams may have hit .406 that year, but who is to say DiMaggio wasn't more important? *He* won the pennant. Williams was MVP in 1949 when he slipped over after a divided vote among many Yankees and when even he will admit he didn't deserve it.

The important things are some of his other actions, still unaccounted for; still really unaccountable:

The day in 1950, first game of a doubleheader—the game long since lost—and Williams is constantly being insulted, berated by those who cherish their left-field perches just to bray at the Kid. He has just hit a grand-slam home run off the glove of Vic Wertz, the ball bouncing into the bullpens which were created to shorten his right-field home run distance. The fans give it to him and he smolders.

Now it is the eighth inning of the second game, Boston leading, 3-1. Williams dropped a fly ball in the first game. In this second game he scurries for Wertz' sinking liner. The ball bounces by him. Williams turns, slowly picks up the ball —permitting three runs to score—and lobs it home. At the end of the inning, the left-field stands are joined by the grandstand. They are giving it to the hero—and giving it to him good.

The Kid—now long since a grown, thinking man—pauses and gives that most obscene of gestures, front, right and left, and then, on batting in the ninth, turns and spits at the fans.

The next day, Yawkey issued a statement of apology. It was the first of many. The moments were many—victory, defeat, batting records, thrown bats, more spitting incidents, many more unknown kindnesses to many people.

There is no point in recounting them all. His personal

charities will never be known. His public events—both the good and the bad—are too well known.

He is a strange man, this Williams. He would be a good man to have for a friend and a bad man to have for an enemy, yet for all those who knew and loved him, for all those who knew and hated him, there was never one person who thought he was the type who would take it out on an enemy and virtually everyone agreed that his major failing was too strong a feeling for his friends.

Let it go which way it will, Ted Williams is quit now.

But he went out with a home run in his final at bat, the most dramatic of them all.

He went out the way he came in.

He was always Williams the First and if they did not win pennants with him, well, then perhaps it was somewhat his fault or, perhaps, it was mostly the fault of others.

No one will ever know. But he played a major role in all of this, from its modern beginnings until his sulk of 1967.

6.

The Country Club

IT IS IMPOSSIBLE to enjoy the game without a scorecard. It is equally impossible to understand the game without a different kind of scorecard—a chart of the musical chairs played in the front offices as men shift back and forth through a maze of intrigues which do better justice to the precepts of Machiavelli.

It is a game some of us treasure and for others it is a business which carries much treasure.

There is cruelty, charm and calculated sportsmanship in the business of major league baseball. The sport changed during the decades of the postwar '40s, '50s and into the '60s. Not just some of the rules. But some of the people. It became a public business with the advent of television and the equal advent of the purchase of the Yankees by CBS. But those who took over the game were no better and no worse than those who had gone before, either the players or the managers or the owners or the executives. It was merely that the world emerged into a new communications era where the game was played before us in our living rooms, where the reporting became less worshipful and more perceptive, where the players became a new and wiser breed, equipped with an organization of their own and equipped with a desire of their own to get, make and keep the money they were worth.

In the final analysis, it is still a slave-trading big business which violates the concept of our constitutional heritage. But it is also the national game; a game which wisely always, you will note, keeps a team in Washington, D.C., and which equally wisely heeds the anger and demands of various Congressmen and Senators whenever the gypsy barons seek to loot one town and move on to another.

A game of complete contrast. We sit in the stands and cheer a sport and they sit in the back rooms and cut up each other and huge piles of money.

This is not intended to be an attack on the virtues of baseball as a sport. But if we are to understand it all—the reasons why we rooted for the impossible dream of 1967 on the one hand and are disillusioned on the other—then we must have a comprehension of the men who run the game. They are precisely like anyone else in what the United States has become. Some good, some bad, some giants, some mental dwarfs. It is a game equally composed of tragedy and humor, of pathos and of greatness, for after all what else could it be? And if it borders on the ridiculous at times, then what else can we expect from a game played by grown men wearing knickers?

Few teams provide a better understanding of what transpired between the end of World War II and 1967. The Red Sox had it all in equal parts. Come now into a new phase, a story of legends, calculated and real, Hall of Famers and heels, moments of truth which for the sheer beauty of combat are irreplaceable and months of despair which are incalculable.

Remember, as well, that this is a sport which gives its supporters heart attacks—"Fan Dies Watching Series"—and hangovers.

So come now into this new phase of the good and bad; the great and the god-awful; watching the progress and the futility of all. Nothing captures the history of baseball like the Red Sox.

Figures.

How else would we have accomplished the impossible dream?

This phase begins in 1947 when Joe Cronin finished third as field manager, third again to the hated Yankees and, exhausted, finally accepted Yawkey's offer of the general manager's office, replacing the ill and dying Eddie Collins, who became vice-president.

Through all the years of watching them and being involved with them; of going away to war and coming back again; of playing bounce ball off a wall pretending to be the Red Sox starting lineup in the late thirties and early forties; of putting down game after game and disappointment after disappointment, the play-by-play box score for a newspaper, and of writing stories about them—through all these years I have never seen a total compilation of the quotes and the facts in chronological order. Working on this book, trying to make it come out on an even basis, calling the shots honestly with neither hero-worship nor disdain, but trying to tell the full complete story of one team and an entire sport (because the Red Sox are a specifically cornerstone/touchstone part of it all)—trying to do all of this, I finally realized that with enough research the truth comes out from their own statements. The history of baseball is written by good men and mediocre men and bad men. It is interesting that we have more of the good men reporting it. The fact that they are in the majority indicates something about the value of a free press and it is also worth considering that the task of being a baseball writer is not always easy; and that those who undertake it often go on into such other sports as war and politics, in the fashion of a Scotty Reston or a Bob Considine. It is a good training ground, this game of baseball.

Few people who have not experienced it will ever understand the true test which being a baseball writer is for the man who must do it for a living; the man who lives from the suitcase, must make quick judgments even at the risk of offending a player or manager friend and, perhaps more importantly, the wrath of an owner if he dares write an uncomplimentary truth—the wrath of an owner which can often extend back to the writer's newspaper where the publisher and the editors will be offended because it is not, finally, precisely whether the truth is told but, more importantly, the all-consuming question of whether the publisher and the editors can still have access to the free and best seats for themselves and their advertisers.

It is a chancy game in many ways and it was gratifying in putting this chapter together that enough research finally brought out all the facts between 1948 and 1967. So I cannot take credit for this chapter. It is instead the compilation of the good reporting of many, many men.

But it is a fascinating one.

Cronin now had moved up front, ultimately heading for the American League President's job. Boston signed Joe McCarthy, colloquially known as "Marse Joe." McCarthy, it can be said with charity, was never a loved man, by his players or by his reporters. But he was respected and feared. It was said of him: "He was the kind of manager who answered questions in such a way that reporters got the idea he did not think the game was in the public interest."

Some of his players were more profane and uncharitable.

Whatever he was, there is no doubt that McCarthy—now in the Hall of Fame and retired on a large farm near Buffalo, New York—was at stage center of baseball for twenty-one years. He was a smart baseball man, with all that the description entails.

A bush-league second baseman—performing at such waystops as Wellsville and Louisville—McCarthy managed three major league teams, winning a pennant with the Cubs in 1929, winning eight more with the Yankees and establishing the dynasty, and losing two in a row with the Red Sox, the first as a result of the 1948 play-off with Cleveland and the second in 1949 when Boston (needing only one victory to clinch it) lost two straight to the Yankees at the Stadium on the last two days of the season, thus giving Casey Stengel his first championship.

McCarthy's career was dotted with the great names of the industry (let us not call it a *sport* in this chapter) and with a long medical history as well, something we will get into shortly.

At Chicago in the National League in 1926, he had Grover Cleveland Alexander, whose fast ball often had an alcohol rub. McCarthy solved the problem by getting rid of Alexander after a wild dispute, trading him to the Cardinals in mid-season, whence Alexander then proceeded to win two games against the Yankees in the World Series and stagger out for the seventh game and—with a one-run lead—strike out Tony Lazzeri with the bases loaded to secure the championship.

In 1929, McCarthy had a future, if controversial, Hall of Fame second baseman named Rogers Hornsby, for whom he traded Alexander in 1926. Hornsby led McCarthy to a pennant, the series lost to the Athletics when McCarthy—Hornsby always claimed—delayed too long in bringing in relief-pitching fast-baller Pat Malone (something to be remembered in light of later Red Sox events). When Malone did get in, Chicago had blown an 8-0 lead, allowing ten runs in one inning, losing 10-8 and losing the series in the next game.

Hornsby was not above intriguing, himself. By September of 1930, he had replaced McCarthy as manager. McCarthy moved over to the Yankees—accepting the talent amassed by Ruppert and ex-Red Sox G.M. Ed Barrow.

McCarthy, despite the string of championships, never won the close ones. It was said that he never won an American League pennant without a coach named Art Fletcher. It was said that he was crotchety and a strong disciplinarian, which would at least be a few votes in his favor. Whatever they did say about him finally, they still voted him into the Hall of Fame. He was the fourteenth Red Sox man to make it.

Whatever they said, then, he was still good enough to make it on their votes, so in the context of baseball "Marse Joe" was a good manager.

And a discontented man.

Casey Stengel, then managing the inept Braves in Boston, remembers one night before WW II when he and McCarthy shared a drawing room on a sleeper-jump back to New York. The Yankees were in first place, as usual. Stengel's Braves, as usual, were seventh.

McCarthy looked out at the flickering farmhouse lights, which dashed in and away, small dots in the rushing black landscape, and said:

"You know, Case. You see that light in the farmhouse over there? That's the life for me. No worries. Nothing to think about except get up and do the milking. Sometimes I think I'm in the greatest business in the world. Then you lose three straight and want to change places with the farmer."

"When the hell did you ever lose three straight?" Stengel asked; the Stengel who would replace McCarthy, beat him and finally drive him into obscurity.

But McCarthy was a good manager. He could handle the likes of Ruth, Lefty Gomez, and Hack Wilson with equal parts of hard-bitten words and understanding. Stengel's style when he took over the Yankees was different. He wasn't always liked either. (Bucky Harris, who had managed the Red Sox and who would come back as Red Sox G.M., had been with Washington, Detroit, Washington, Detroit again in this vast game of musical chairs, and was exceedingly popular when he took over the Yankees from McCarthy in 1947 and 1948. Stengel was more caustic. A sample remark in '49: "How many of you guys own stock in the New York Central?

Good. Buy more. You'll be riding it to the bushes tomorrow.")

He could be understanding of men like Lou Gehrig. It was April 30, 1939. Relief pitcher Johnny Murphy, the first of the famous Yankee "firemen" and later the farm director who presided over the demise of the Red Sox before moving to the Mets to establish an even more ludicrous chapter, watched Gehrig make a routine play against Washington and said:

"Nice going, Lou."

Gehrig came to McCarthy and said: "Joe, when that happens, it's time for me to quit."

Gehrig was gone. McCarthy was saddened, because he was also a man who could feel deep hurts; saddened on the one hand, angry at some of his upstart, roughhouse players, but still charmed by them sometimes—such as Gomez, the wild "Lefty" who could be the man for the moment when Gehrig, soon to die, returned to the Yankees clubhouse, a wan, brave man; the players all confused, not knowing what to say—or McCarthy either for that matter—and Gomez reached over and picked up a soup bone with which the players used to hone their bats and said:

"Hey, Lou. You think you got a bad deal from those doctors? Look what they took out of my throwing arm."

One of the better moments of baseball.

McCarthy lasted through the original, founding dynasty of the Yankees, breaking Miller Huggins' pennant record (six) with his eight and, ultimately, beating Huggins into the Hall of Fame.

He admired DiMaggio, Gehrig and few others and the Yankees won for him until May of 1946 when—as the Red Sox embarked on their first modern pennant under the direction of Cronin—McCarthy suddenly quit.

It came after an argument with Larry MacPhail, a dispute which raged for several days, winding up in a locked suite, which was also part of the mystique of McCarthy. The breakup came in a Yankee Stadium game against Cleveland. Bill Zuber threw a home run ball and McCarthy stomped through the dugout. On the plane to Detroit that night he turned his rage against Joe Page, his newest fireman, and after a period in his hotel suite it was announced by the Yankees that "Marse Joe" McCarthy was suffering from dyspepsia. He returned to his Buffalo farm and Bill Dickey became interim manager.

Baseball writers must be students of medicine as well as part-time psychologists and, occasionally, physical defenders of their beliefs (this last is when portable typewriters come in handy). Writers must know all the terms for sudden "attacks" of dyspepsia, ulcers, gall bladder, plain general stomachaches and pleurisy, ailments which have suddenly stricken more managers than hard dugout seats, hot days in St. Louis and bad traveling hours.

McCarthy was gone. So were the Yankees temporarily.

For 1946 was the year of the Red Sox; one of the finest teams for this one season which was ever assembled. Even if they staggered a little near the end, flipping and flopping like a wounded flounder, toting their champagne from town to town until they finally *did* clinch the inevitable pennant.

Inevitably, they played the Cardinals. There is no point to recount the whole story. Williams failed to hit up to his standard, although he was faulted more than was necessary. He did *bunt* one day in a losing cause, to the eternal chagrin of Joe Garagiola, a kid just up and cocky. Garagiola was 4-for-4 for the Cards. "I thought at long last I was going to get my name in the papers," he said. "But the next day all the headlines said: 'Williams Bunts.' "

Testimony to what the last of the .406 hitters meant to this game.

The best pitching staff in baseball—Tex Hughson, Dave Ferriss, Joe Dobson—couldn't hold back the Cards of Musial and Schoendienst and Slaughter, and the three victories of Harry "the Cat" Brecheen culminated in St. Louis that day when St. Louis won it all, 4-3, and when Johnny Pesky inadvertently held the ball a split second too long as Slaughter scored the deciding run by circling the bases from first (and ignoring the third base coach's stop sign) on a weak double, the Country Boy becoming forever a new part of the baseball legend.

Pesky didn't hear the yell of Mike Higgins, the third baseman signed on down the stretch to help the team with his poise (and he did help, because Hig was a very good third baseman). Bobby Doerr was playing second—the best second baseman in the American League for many years—and each of these men, as well as Williams and Cronin, would have an involvement in what transpired in the future of the Red Sox front office.

But that is getting ahead of the musical chairs game up front. The action on the field slowed, scuttled in disappointment and chagrin at the loss to St. Louis; and after finishing third to Bucky Harris' championship Yankees in 1947, Cronin moved up to G.M.

Yawkey, already laying plans through that season, had secured McCarthy at $50,000-plus per year. Marse Joe's dyspepsia was cured and he joined the team for 1948. The talk was pennant. The Red Sox still were the best of all. The talk was also personalities. Could McCarthy handle the ego of Ted Williams?

McCarthy said, "When I can't get along with a .400 hitter, then it's time to quit."

His first move was to send a Red Sox pitcher named Bill Zuber down to Louisville.

Zuber? Right. The same pitcher who with the Yankees in 1946 threw the gopher ball which set McCarthy into the tantrum which cost his job.

McCarthy and Cronin made a strengthening deal, collecting shortstop Vern Stephens and pitchers Ellis Kinder and Jack Kramer from the St. Louis Browns. Pesky was moved to third. It could be the year of the pennant again. McCarthy was a miracle worker. Right?

Well. Maybe.

He knew he had his hands full. During his first Boston press conference the full—and unnecessary—furor of the Ted Williams' "Baby Incident" was underway. The trade with the Browns promised certain troubles. Stephens, Kinder, and Kramer had almost gone to Cleveland for Lou Boudreau, a trade which the master hustler Bill Veeck almost pulled off in an attempt to get rid of Boudreau. Instead, Boston bought the three men for $250,000—a good move—but Kinder, for one, was well enough known for his habits that he hadn't made the majors until he was in his thirties. Stephens and Kramer had tempers. And there was the matter of the big temper, Williams.

McCarthy was a man of conservative dress. Williams wouldn't wear a tie. McCarthy solved that problem by showing up for spring training in a vivid sports shirt. Age brings its wisdom and concessions. Williams played well for McCarthy.

Most players usually did. He liked fighting ballplayers. He made no excuse for quitters. He missed New York and he missed men like DiMaggio. But he put his whole mind to it in these last two great years of the Red Sox and they began a run for the pennant, while across Commonwealth Avenue the Boston Braves of Billy Southworth made a run for the National League—Southworth, an old rival, nemesis and a man who was not respected by the Braves at all; just plain and sheerly hated to the point where the *Mutiny on the Manatee* would develop at a later spring training.

McCarthy had a new rookie, Billy Goodman. And patience. He handled the flare-ups. Vern Stephen swung at a pitch over his head and McCarthy yelled at him. Stephens turned and swore. When he returned from the dugout the players waited for the explosion. Instead, McCarthy sat Stephens down, put an arm around him and said, "You shouldn't swear at me, son. I'm here to help you."

He had arguments with umpires, gave Matt Batts a lecture on catching in public. (Some people said he kicked him in the pants, but McCarthy insisted he was kicking dirt at the umpire. Batts didn't say.)

It was the year of Veeck and Boudreau at Cleveland, and McCarthy in Boston, and they flew to the wire through a world of bench jockeying and turmoil, men yelling to Dom DiMaggio, "Hey, headwaiter, what's on the menu?" . . . to Pesky, "Hey, you gonna hit the ball with that nose?" . . . and more profane statements to others like Tebbetts and Williams.

The first play-off in American League history resulted. McCarthy's good starting staff expected the assignment. Instead, he picked Denny Galehouse, creating one of baseball's lasting controversies.

Boudreau saw Galehouse warming up on the Fenway Park sidelines and told a coach, "McCarthy's faking us. He's got somebody else warming up under the stands. Put on your topcoat and run down under right field and see if Parnell or someone isn't warming up."

It was no fake. Galehouse was the man. The way it turned out, no one would have stopped the bats of Boudreau, Ken Keltner and Joe Gordon. Cleveland went with Gene Bearden, a knuckle ball pitcher, who was winning his twentieth game. Bearden was so nervous he had a concealed drink on the bench. This was not considered unusual on the dissension-ridden Indians and it was said that after the game the champagne victory celebration included Bearden popping Boudreau.

Interesting. Boudreau would preside over part of the demise of the Red Sox as their manager a few years hence, driving Dom DiMaggio out of baseball as well.

But this was the year of the Indians. Bearden became one of the series heroes. The next season he was nothing. Owner Bill Veeck explained why:

"His knuckler was his pitch. His saver. But it broke low. Casey Stengel had him at Oakland when we brought him up. I asked Casey about him and he said he was okay. He was. But the next year Stengel was managing the Yankees. He knew about Bearden and he just told his batters to wait him out. He'd get behind the hitter with the knuckler and then have to throw the fast ball or the curve. Goodbye. But Casey didn't blow the whistle in 1948. He wasn't in the big league."

Veeck left town with a World Series won from the Braves' only hope of "Spahn and Sain and pray for rain," leaving behind a personal opinion of his manager. "Lou," he said, "is a lousy manager. But I'm stuck with him until I can unload him gracefully."

Now, it was 1949, the last great year for the Red Sox until 1967, a 160-day, 148-game pursuit of the New York Yankees of Charles Dillon Stengel. McCarthy showed the strain of it. Before a Fourth of July doubleheader in Philadelphia he said one night at dinner, "I hope my nerves hold out. Connie Mack always said to watch your nerves. He said after he won in 1910 and 1911 he almost went nuts in 1912."

He said a few days later, "I'm disgusted. It's not my kind of team. Six or seven of them are all stars. But they're not my kind." Years later, he left Ted Williams off his personal all-time All Star team.

McCarthy was a man for sitting in a darkened suite, thinking, worrying and comforted by a "jar of the creature."

On July 17, 1949, there was a rumor his contract options would not be picked up, that he might be immediately replaced and that Mike Higgins—Yawkey's pal—was coming up from Birmingham.

McCarthy rallied himself and his team, surviving the return of Joe DiMaggio to the Yankees and finally seizing first place, coming into Yankee Stadium for the final two games of the year needing only one victory to clinch the pennant.

Mel Parnell, who had won 25 games, left after four innings. Joe Dobson finally was faced with pitching to Johnny Lindell as Stengel juggled, trying to make the decision whether to hit with Lindell or Charlie Keller. He went with Lindell and Lindell hit the game-winning home run off Dobson.

Now there was one game.

McCarthy went with his other ace, Ellis Kinder, on Sunday. Saturday night some of the players came to Kinder's buddy, Artie Richman of the old *Daily Mirror*. "Take him out on the town," they said. "We want our regular Eli out there. Don't let him stay sober tonight."

Kinder—like Alexander—was a man for all seasons in the clutch, a man with ice water (or something) in his veins as he faced the Yankees. Rizzuto opened with a triple, the drive bouncing trickily around the left-field fence while Williams scrambled after it. He scored the only run and in the eighth Kinder, pitching superbly, trailed 1-0, the Red Sox at bat. McCarthy had to make the decision. He put in a pinch hitter, Tom Wright, a young kid just up from Louisville, used because McCarthy was gambling that the Yanks would not have a book on him; a left-hander for whom the Stadium's right-field wall was a perfect target. But Raschi walked him and caused Dom DiMaggio to hit into a double play.

McCarthy had to use Parnell in relief—the same Parnell who would broadcast the Red Sox games of 1967. Parnell was hit hard. Henrich homered. Hughson came in. Coleman blooped a double past Zarilla. The Yanks scored four runs. It was a second pennant in a row for Stengel.

McCarthy, waving off criticism for his decision to relieve Kinder, denied he would quit and took the train home with his team. "I'm not running out on them now."

It was the end of an era, however. The beginning of a long drought. The decade of the '50s was beginning. The Red Sox had characters like Kinder and his sidekick, their first singing pitcher, Maurice McDermott, and tantrums and temperament.

Cronin signed former Detroit Tigers manager Steve O'Neill as supervisor of scouts in the Midwest in January, 1949, and all through that 1949 season O'Neill was ready to step in as manager if something went wrong with McCarthy in one of those darkened suites. Yawkey wanted Higgins, but Cronin had no great affection for Higgins, no great desire to make a field manager of the boss' best friend. (There is a natural law of self-preservation among general managers.) O'Neill was Cronin's man.

Everyone knew McCarthy was going. The Red Sox were eight and a half games behind the Yankees, stuck in third place behind the second-place Tigers. They lost five in a row to Cleveland and Detroit, and McCarthy didn't show up for the last game. The team moved to Chicago, June 22, and McCarthy was still incommunicado in his suite. The phones were buzzing. A vicious argument raged between McCarthy, Cronin, and Yawkey.

At 1:30 it was announced that McCarthy had come down with a bad case of "pleurisy" and would go home to Buffalo for a rest. Steve O'Neill would manage the team for a few days. McCarthy told his best newspaper friend, a Buffalo sports editor, "No. I'm not finished. I need the rest. I've been assured I have the job," hung up the phone and took a plane home to Buffalo. By the time he landed at the airport O'Neill had been announced as the permanent manager and McCarthy was taking a swing at a photographer. "Pleurisy," that time-honored ailment which afflicts baseball managers suddenly, had struck again.

Birdie Tebbetts said, "It's a strange business. It took the death of Kiki Cuyler to get O'Neill a coaching job and now he's the manager. It's a ticklish situation. The less said the better." Tebbetts, who would go on to manage and become a general manager, had reason to be concerned. He was McCarthy's "man" on this team. He was ticketed to be gone.

Stephens, whose temper had clashed with McCarthy's, said, "He was a good manager, but he was getting old."

McCarthy several months later said, "I didn't quit. I retired. When you start to read late at night with the lights out something is wrong."

O'Neill, Yawkey, Cronin, said, "We'll win more than we lose." That wasn't quite true. The demise was on. Boston staggered along in third. For years sportswriters speculated about what happened when McCarthy was with the Red Sox. This chapter appears to make it obvious—the Red Sox gave him "pleurisy."

Tebbetts was sold to the Indians in midwinter. O'Neill—faced with Ted Williams' elbow ailment down the stretch in 1950 and throughout 1951—tried to bring some semblance of order to his squad. But they still finished third in 1951 and halfway through the year everyone knew it didn't matter anyway—O'Neill, who also lived outside Buffalo, would soon be neighborly with McCarthy. The cliques grew worse and Jerry Nason suggested that what the Red Sox needed was not a manager but a registered psychiatrist. The *Globe* sports editor made a sound point in September, 1951:

"Joe Cronin couldn't do it—except when he caught the league with its slip showing in the abnormal year of 1946.

"Joe McCarthy couldn't do it. O'Neill can't do it—maybe. And Lou Boudreau isn't going to be able to do it, either.

"The only one who CAN do it is Tom Yawkey, whose patience has been exceeded only by the generosity with which he has rewarded failure.

"What has been the matter with the Red Sox all these bitter years is a state of mind, the absence of a philosophy and the presence of a ruinous sophistication. What the Red Sox need now is a rowdy, a guy from the other side of the tracks. A guy like Durocher would have them hating his guts—and winning."

It was generally agreed that this was an accurate summation, one which would not reach fruition until 1967 when Williams the Second came along.

Meanwhile, Boudreau was made manager and O'Neill was on the Buffalo shuffle. Lou brought in "the Youth Movement," which was another way of saying that Yawkey laid out a fortune to try to rebuild a disaster. Boudreau finished sixth in 1952 and fourth in 1953 and 1954.

In 1951 he signed up saying, "There are no untouchables. Not even Ted Williams." He went to his first spring training camp in 1952 and sent pitcher Parnell home to Boston and accused Parnell, McDermott and Kinder of "jaking it." He tried to handle Jimmy Piersall in the poor kid's first season and booted it badly. After Piersall slapped Stephens' kid in the locker room (which admittedly was not the most sensible action), Boudreau sent him back to Birmingham to "prevent a serious incident." Piersall was in trouble. He had a mental condition. Everyone knew that. He was in fights with his teammates, including a beauty with McDermott, and with his opponents, most notably Billy Martin, who surfaces again in this book as a Twins coach in 1967. Boudreau switched him from the outfield to shortstop which made the kid more nervous. Cronin and Yawkey demonstrated great kindness and care for Piersall. The same could not be said of his treatment by Boudreau.

And the Red Sox were just breaking up. Veeck was right in one thing. Boudreau was a great shortstop. He made a beautiful appearance and was a fine, upstanding man. But he couldn't manage. Particularly this team. The front office didn't help. The scouting staffs were filled with retainers living off Yawkey's generosity: old ballplayers, nice guys, but not scouts. And they were laying out money for Boudreau and

Cronin's youth movement. Huge sums of money. Check some of these:

Jerry Mallett—$75,000
Marty Keough—$100,000
Frank Baumann—$86,000
Jerry Zimmerman—$75,000
Billy Consolo—$65,000
Don Buddin—$45,000
Jim Pagliaroni—$75,000

Admittedly, this was in the days of the big bonuses, but this was preposterous. Branch Rickey, Jr.—more regularly known as "the Twig"—who bid in the same competitive markets said, "Yawkey spent over $3,000,000. I know. We were bidding against him sometimes, but we stopped way short. Everyone took Yawkey. And for a fortune."

The Red Sox even paid $50,000 to some kid named Al Moran, who was never seen at Fenway Park. Probably the only good investment they did make was $75,000 for a catcher named Haywood Sullivan, but he hurt his back and never was much. But at least they got to know him and brought him back in 1966 as director of player personnel, one more step toward the 1967 impossible dream.

Meanwhile it was a nightmare. Boudreau, who had achieved much publicity with his Williams shift in 1946, changed his mind and his game from minute to minute, lifting catchers instead of pitchers, batting Williams second and pitchers high on the roster, shifting outfielders for one hitter.

It was supposed to be the "New Breed" of baseball and the "Youth Movement." Both stank. A foul word, but the most accurate description.

It was weird and goofy baseball and the established stars, such as Vic Wertz and Dom DiMaggio, grew to hate Boudreau. DiMaggio quit in May, 1953, when he learned that Boudreau was cutting him up the back. The great ones were going fast. The intrigues between the locker room and the front office grew. Yet, Boudreau had lasted three high-paying years. He even had an extra year to go when he was fired in 1954 and when he left he was unconcerned. Arnold Johnson had hired him as the first manager of the new Kansas City Athletics. "We want the best we can get," Johnson said. Boudreau was fired, resigned, whatever in mid-season 1957 at Kansas City.

Meanwhile, back at the house of cards, the palace of coups d'état, the membership of the country club was growing. By 1954 Michael F. "Pinky" Higgins could no longer be withstood. Regardless, Boudreau's extra year had to be paid off. Higgins had won the Little World Series at Louisville. He appeared to be an excellent manager and had legitimate offers from Paul Richards. That is the best way to get into the big league, of course. You get the offer, or some talk of one, contact the parent team and tell them you have an offer and shaky stands the head of the current resident big league manager. It is as much a ground rule of the game as balls and strikes.

Besides, Hig probably had to be better than Boudreau. It was "time for a change" and Hig was Yawkey's pal. Williams —Ted, that is—was also feuding with Boudreau, one of the few times when all sportswriters concurred with him. That clinched it. Yawkey called Cronin from his South Carolina plantation on Sunday, October 10.

Cronin called Boudreau. Higgins arrived in Boston for an announcement conference on October 11, 1954. He was well and pleasantly greeted. The renaissance had arrived. The Youth Movement was dead. Some soul asked Cronin what Boudreau's response was when he was called on Sunday to be told he was fired. Cronin said, "You know how Lou is. He was more concerned about some water in his cellar. They have a flood out there."

There should be room for that statement as a streamer on the Red Sox battle flag. It sums up three years, 1952-53-54.

Bucky Harris, whom Yawkey had fired in 1934 as part of the palace coup of Eddie Collins, signed on to manage Detroit for two years. The resident geniuses of the American League were Stengel and Al Lopez in Cleveland. Higgins wasn't that far behind. He was a pleasant man, a calm, conservative manager; he had played on winners and, at least, he *knew* baseball. He had what became a nervous affliction for the fans—he really thought Don Buddin, the bonus boy who played well for him at Louisville, was a major league shortstop. It is conservatively estimated that the Red Sox lost 100,000 fans who quit in disgust after steadily watching Buddin fail.

But Hig wasn't that bad. Things weren't that desperate. The big guy, Williams, could still hit. There were some very capable players and a few good ones, and although their runs at the leaders were sometimes thought halfhearted, Higgins managed to finish 4-4-3-3 over the next four seasons.

The underlying fact, however, was that it was still a poor team without leadership. Higgins' contract was renewed after three years on September 21, 1958—a date more notable because it was the day Williams hit Cronin's poor housekeeper in the head with his tossed bat.

But the lethargy existed.

Yawkey's team was in trouble and Yawkey is no fool. He may have been victimized, may have been too generous, but he was trying. He had plans to move Joe Cronin into the presidency of the American League when Will Harridge retired in 1959 and he needed someone who could perk up the front office. He turned again in 1957 to Bucky Harris, no longer with Detroit, perhaps out of an old feeling of kinship for Bucky and perhaps because he felt guilty about the firing after the 1934 season.

At lower levels, one Richard O'Connell was demonstrating staying power as a new kind of baseball executive, learning it from the ground up both as a business and a sport, and some of the scouts weren't doing that badly, led by Neal Mahoney and Botts Nekola. But their time was still far distant.

The Yankee dynasty was still intact, even though Ralph Houk was doing his best to undermine Stengel, whose repetitious championships were now making the American League a bore.

That was another of the troubles. The National League was interesting. Somehow, as television grew stronger and stronger so had the National League. It had tang, taste, flavor.

The Red Sox were becoming virtually a forgotten team. The same old statements were made each spring training. The same old finishes—in the first division, but not really a big money threat, not a winner.

The appointment of Harris as Cronin's assistant was not a happy experience for Higgins. Cronin wasn't that pleased either, but he could live with it. The presidency of the American League wasn't that far away. Hig had more troubles. He was just the manager, hoping to be general manager, and now there was a familiar old figure in the way—Harris.

On February 1, 1959, the traditional All American saga and success story was completed. From the sandlots to the ultimate. Cronin replaced Harridge, receiving a seven-year appointment. Harris seven days earlier was officially appointed Red Sox general manager.

Musical chairs was continuing. But Higgins' days were marked.

During the winter the grapevine indicated that Ted Williams might take over. The name of Eddie Stanky came up.

Ralph Houk was mentioned. Even Pee Wee Reese, the shortstop who got away in the Louisville deal so long, long ago. It was logical to assume that Harris would be after Higgins. And it was equally logical to assume that Higgins hadn't been around baseball this long without creating a few savers of his own. In point of fact, he was a good manager, except for his thing about young Buddin. He'd planned on dumping Billy Klaus in 1956, but the guy played so well at shortstop that they couldn't. ("At least not this year," Klaus said then. "I've been around long enough to know how to take care of myself.") They had the Parnell no-hitter against Chicago at Fenway in 1956—the first no-hitter by a Red Sox pitcher in thirty-three years, or since Howard Ehmke did it in 1923.

Hurrah. Things weren't so bad.

There was this troublesome allusion to the fact that the Red Sox didn't have any Negro players—the last team in the majors to have such a boycott—but Harris, Higgins, and Yawkey all vigorously denied this in slightly Southern drawls, even pointing back to a 1957 interview in which Cronin predicted that Boston would have a couple "of them" in a year or two. The best two candidates were an infielder named Pumpsie Green ("*They* all do have funny names, don't *they?*" a Red Sox executive said) and a pitcher named Earl Wilson. Wilson went into the Marines for two years, but the pressure was so great for some kind of at least token Negro that Green was brought up to spring training in 1959 at Scottsdale. (I mean, every large corporation has to have *their* Negro, right?)

Green led the team in batting during spring training, but was sent back down to Minneapolis. The NAACP and other agencies interested in possible discrimination asked some nasty questions of the Red Sox, who had the usual answers, including a public statement before committee by O'Connell (who handled it better than anyone else) and a statement by Harris, who showed that the Red Sox had "five of them in our minors." A hasty recount by Harris' chief scout, Johnny Murphy, showed that there were actually seven Negroes spread through the chain and the good intent and high interest of the Red Sox in always seeking talent concluded: "Why we've even had scouts look at Joe Cronin's kid. They decided they'd rather have the old man."

But it was not humorous. The fact of the matter was that the Red Sox were discriminatory and that Higgins was particularly so. Green was a tragic victim of the last barrier in baseball. At Scottsdale that spring training of 1959 he was not permitted to live with the Red Sox in their own plush hotels, instead being placed in the Adams Hotel in Phoenix, 17 miles away.

Green was used to it. He had expected it. The Adams Hotel wasn't as bad as the first one the Red Sox put him in. At least, at the Adams he had Negro players from the Giants. Not bad players either—Willie Mays, Orlando Cepeda, Willie McCovey.

Before that, Green had been met by traveling secretary Tom Dowd at the airport and placed in the Frontier Motel, so far from everything in Phoenix that he lived completely alone, talking to no one, eating alone, reading himself to sleep at night, being picked up by a car in the morning and driven to Scottsdale and the car dropping him back off at night—not even being given a car for himself in a delicate situation such as this.

The days at the park were all right. The players did not discriminate. Ted Williams and others treated him well. But everyone knew. It was automatic that Pumpsie would not stay with Higgins' team. And he was sent down as the Red Sox headed east.

The fact of the matter was that he probably did need more seasoning and in point of fact he never was that good a big league ballplayer. But the Red Sox had muffed things up again, alibiing with everyone who regarded it as an alibi. The front office tried to convince everyone that they had tried to trade for Al Smith of Chicago or Charlie Neal of the Dodgers. Some believed it. Some did not. (It was true, however.)

But it was bungled again.

The next thing to bungle followed logically. How not to fire a losing manager. The Red Sox were comfortably nestled in last place in Washington on July 1, riding the crest of a four-game losing streak.

The way Bucky Harris told it, Tom Yawkey called him in Philadelphia where the general manager was attending an interleague trading meeting. "Yawkey said, 'Aren't you in the wrong town?'

"I took the hint," Harris continued, "and went to Washington."

His arrival signaled trouble for Higgins and the press speculated that it might be the end. Higgins didn't talk with Harris in Washington where the Red Sox managed to lose three straight. Harris left and went to Baltimore to await the arrival of the team. Whatever anyone else was planning, Harris had the ax out for Hig all right. He'd made arrangements with Griffith to talk to the Senators' coach, Billy Jurges, after first attempting to talk Red Sox coach Del Baker, an old friend, into taking the manager's job. Baker refused. Somewhere in the background, Harris also talked to his old buddy, Ralph Houk, a man also respected by Yawkey. The Senators were now in New York for a holiday series and Jurges knew he was at least in the zone of consideration, confessing to columnist Bob Addie that "nothing will probably come of it, but I know the Red Sox are asking about me."

Now the byways and secret paths of baseball are not always known. This palace coup has to be put together carefully. Here is Harris in Baltimore having made his plans. Yawkey is in Boston. The press says Higgins will be fired. On the night of July 2 the Red Sox arrive in Baltimore, and Higgins and Harris go to a late dinner. By midnight, Higgins has re-

Jimmy Piersall, the gallant Red Sox outfielder who overcame a nervous disorder, meets with then Senator John F. Kennedy.

Piersall had less pleasant words for the umpire in one of his typical outbursts over a called strike.

Mike Higgins, left, was blamed for the disorganization of the Red Sox. John Pesky was one of his victims as a manager.

Higgins was a strong manager before he tired. Here he passes the "word" to Umpire Larry Napp.

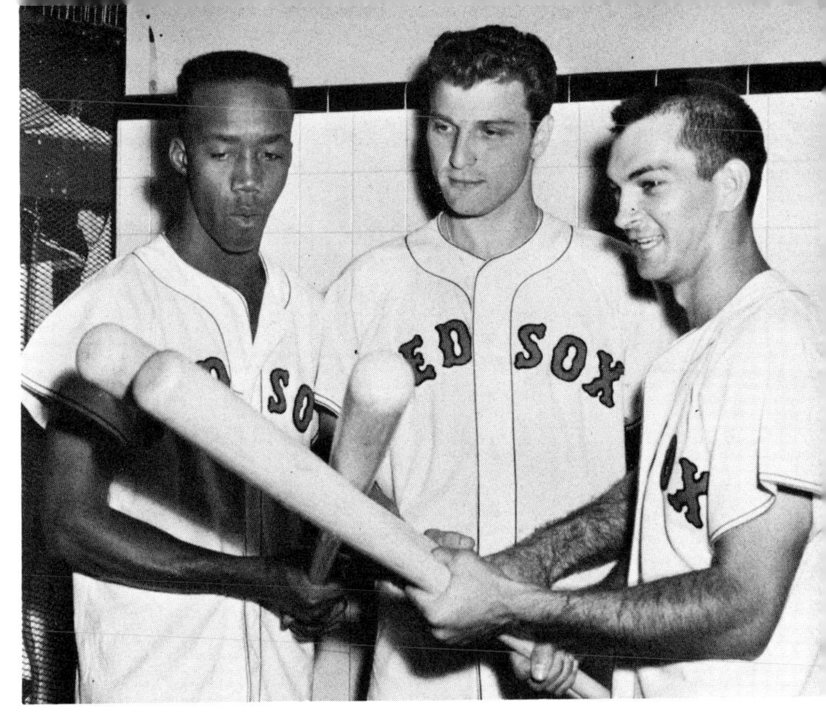

Pumpsie Green, Jerry Casale, and Don Buddin were three young Sox hopefuls who just didn't pan out during the last-place period.

Shortstop Don Buddin was Higgins' "boy," but he never made it as a major leaguer although he was in the lineup for years.

Green and Higgins look somber, and there was a good reason. Higgins had just fined him for his absence on "Bethlehem" attempted trip with Gene Conley.

Higgins was a top-rated player with many A.L. teams and was impressive when he first joined Sox from Connie Mack's Athletics in 1937.

fused to be fired until he can talk to Yawkey. "He hired me and only he can personally fire me."

By morning, Rudy York was appointed acting manager and Higgins held court in the hotel with a parade of his players passing through. "It looks like a wake," someone said.

"It is of sorts," Higgins said. "Managers never quit, remember that. They only get fired." He seemed relaxed enough and teased his temporary replacement, York, saying, "Don't tell them about your managing record at North Platte, Rudy."

Yawkey meanwhile assembled an extraordinary press conference at Fenway Park—the first he had ever called. He proceeded to lash the press for causing all of this trouble ("Can't I send the general manager to see the team without having it seem as though the manager is fired?").

Higgins played for Cronin before they both moved into front office and began musical chairs game as team faltered into second division.

In the middle of Yawkey's press conference, some of the reporters were notified that Harris had announced in Baltimore the appointment of Billy Jurges as the new manager.

The total effect of this on Yawkey will never really be known. He was informed of the name of his new manager in the middle of his own press conference, politely wished him every success and then sealed Harris' doom by talking about Higgins. "Firing him was the hardest thing I have ever had to do. He was the first manager I ever personally hired. It all began after the World Series on the train home. I asked him if he wanted to stay in baseball as an executive. He impressed me becase he wanted to go down and start from the ground up. He did a fine job in the minors and he did a fine job in the majors. I feel very badly about this."

Meanwhile, back at the ball park, Jurges was a name which evoked dim images in the minds of men accustomed to the American League. He was a coach or something for the Senators, right? A good National League player, though.

Jurges had been more than just good. He was one of the best shortstops the Cubs ever had, playing alongside Billy Herman and making a great double play combination. He was also a fierce competitor. He hurt his arm. He hurt his knee. He suffered a nearly fatal beaning. Yet he still came back. He played on three pennant winners and made three hits in the third game of the World Series against the Yankees in 1932. He also made a fielding gem, retiring Joe Sewell. But who was the next batter? Babe Ruth. And this was the famous game where Ruth pointed the spot of his home run and then hit it off the pitch of Charlie Root.

That was Jurges' luck.

Now, he had the last-place Red Sox. Jurges was a particularly fine man in the opinion of everyone who ever knew him. It is popularly known in baseball and by the public that he was shot in the ribs and hand by a girl in 1932 over a case of unrequited love. Less popularly known is the fact that Jurges

—single at the time—actually was trying to be the peacemaker between the girl and a married player. He stepped between and got shot.

That was Jurges' luck, too.

Years after Jurges was fired, his second-base sidekick, Herman, known in the league as "Higgins' man," would use Jurges' courage as an illustration to a lack of stamina by Rico Petrocelli, saying:

"I saw Jurges get shot and come back and play two weeks later. Petrocelli would be out with a sore throat that long."

But this was 1959 and no one was feeling that pleasantly about Jurges, the unwitting interloper. Higgins was permitted to depart on what Yawkey announced would be an extended vacation, after which he would rejoin the front office.

Jurges took over what he thought was a ball club and expressed himself in the first team meeting: "I don't like dogs," he said. "I like fighters."

The speech worked well enough to present the Red Sox with five straight victories over the Yankees at the Stadium. Jurges was a miracle worker for one series. He came home and lost a game and was booed. He was confused and the confusing Red Sox quickly recovered their stride and settled back toward the bottom again.

Higgins had left his mark on the team and on some of those on the edges of it. No one was really going to tolerate too much from Jurges and he was just too honest, too involved, too pleased with having his first big league team to realize it. Ted Williams, to his credit, did nothing to injure Jurges' chances. But Williams was always a loner, not a leader. There was an internal feud between him and Jackie Jensen. Jensen was the Most Valuable Player of 1958. Williams was the batting champion (.328). How then, one wonders, did the team suddenly fall so low, in one season? It had been coming for a long time. The factions had grown. Jensen, troubled with other problems, terrified to fly and undergoing psychiatric treatment, held out for more money before the season, arguing he was worth as much as Williams. Harris publicly blamed the whole matter on "the Williams thing."

This carried over to the disorganization of the coup d'état and Jurges simply couldn't cope with it. But he tried. He brought Pumpsie Green up on July 22 in Chicago, putting him at shortstop for Don Buddin, Higgins' favored player.

Green was a second baseman. "Do you need a shortstop?" Jurges was asked. "Buddin's thumb is hurt," Jurges said tactfully. The ploy failed. Buddin had too much strength going for him. Hig wasn't out of the Red Sox picture. He was just vacationing.

They traveled over to Kansas City amidst an uproar on a story by Ed Rummil of the *Christian Science Monitor,* who quoted "an established star."

The star told Rummil:

"Everyone is just going through the motions. Nobody will try for this guy."

Forthright Jurges called a team meeting with the press attending. Said Jurges:

"If this player is so smart he should be general manager. I challenge him to stand up here right now and say the same things." Receiving no answer, he then got into a dispute with the press. That certainly didn't advance his stature, evidence of the continuing breakdown of all communication now. It went from bad to worse. Jurges never lived down a statement he made to player Pete Daley, whom he called back as Daley went up to hit against the Yanks' Ryne Duren.

"All he said to me was: 'Watch him, Pete. He's quick,' " Daley told everyone who would listen. The players didn't want to give him a chance. Jensen, a pleasant enough man but enormously troubled, came into the final game of the season leading Rocky Colavito of the Indians by one run in the RBI derby. Jensen asked permission of Jurges to leave early and went home to California. "I'm not interested in the title," he said, "I'm in this for the money."

The Indians, calling Fenway to find out how Jensen was doing, so shocked Colavito when they told him that he pressed and didn't drive in a run, and Jensen won the title anyway. Making matters even worse, Buddin and Jurges got into a shouting match in the dugout on the same day. Buddin fostered ill feeling throughout the second half of the season ("What does he think I am, a little-leaguer? Who needs practice?"—this to one of the National League's greatest shortstops). On this final day, Buddin hit a three-run homer and Jurges came forward to congratulate him. Buddin let fly with some vitriolic comments. Jurges answered, "Well, at least I won't have to put up with you much longer."

The Red Sox finished fifth, not a bad showing considering where Jurges started from. Higgins was signed on as executive assistant to Bucky Harris (ah, uneasy lies the head which wears the general manager's crown) and Jurges went home to Washington to sell Christmas trees. It was the last season of goodwill he was to know, for 1960 was a complete and planned disaster.

In 1960, Jurges brought up Billy Herman and Sal Maglie, coaches who would be involved—or coming back through the revolving door of the front offices—in the year of the impossible dream.

He tried to make some other moves, which didn't come off. The Red Sox front office traded Sammy White to Cleveland for Russ Nixon, a trade which was called off when White wouldn't go and quit baseball, and Jurges entered spring training with one Haywood Sullivan, the $75,000 bonus boy, as his catcher; the same Sullivan who would become director of player personnel for the 1967 Red Sox.

Sullivan had a bad back and had squatted in the Red Sox dugout without work during the Higgins regime.

Pitcher Frank Sullivan—a blithe, free spirit—had a solid reason why Higgins did not play Haywood Sullivan. "He doesn't know he's on the team," Frank said. Sully, an ex-combat infantryman in Korea, a good pitcher who went bad under the tutelage of the Red Sox administration, always kept his wit. It was he who best summed up the entire period of the wayward Red Sox. It was one night when the Red Sox were dawdling along, sinking lower and lower, and flying home to Boston through a thunderstorm. As lightning flashed around the plane, Sullivan leaned over and said to writer Larry Claflin:

"This team is insured for $2,000,000. Sort of makes you wonder which way Mr. Yawkey is rooting, doesn't it?"

Whether Yawkey was rooting at all during 1960 is unknown. Certainly, Jurges had little aid. He became more frustrated, made whipping boys out of some, tried to trade, tried to fine, tried to curfew, tried to command and kept falling further behind in the standings. His hair grew white. By late May, G.M. Harris was giving Jurges a vote of confidence. (In baseball this is tantamount to public acknowledgment that a new manager is on the way.)

"Let's give Jurges a break," Harris said. "I've managed more teams than anyone in baseball. I've had clubs which lost ten in a row. Let's not throw a weight on this man's neck and drown him."

Five days later—and you think the Dodgers were daffy?—Jurges was giving Harris and Yawkey a vote of confidence. As usual, Jurges tried to do the forthright thing and got in trouble for it. The Red Sox were in Washington and Jurges flew off the handle at a writer, saying many things, including that his hands were tied by the front office. Harris called Jurges who called a press conference to apologize. Beautiful. Baseball at its best.

Three days after that Harris gave Jurges his second vote of confidence. The Red Sox came back from a 3-11 road trip.

Ted Williams, using Associated Press writer Joe Reichler as his vehicle (as he often did in his continuing vendetta against the Boston writers), stated: "I don't want to be a manager. Especially, I don't want to be a manager in Boston." (That may have been the wisest decision he ever made.)

Yawkey was in his office and unavailable. Years later, Yawkey would admit he never did offer the manager's job to Williams. "He was just too volatile. He needed to settle down before he could be a manager."

Armed with this vote of confidence, Jurges voted for himself four days later, saying he was sure there was no dissension on his club. On June 8, Jurges wasn't feeling well. "I ate some goulash," he said. The Red Sox suggested he see an internist. The internist found Jurges nervous and rundown. By the time Jurges got back to the park to tell Harris and Yawkey, the Red Sox had already made an announcement. It was time for a change. Jurges would take a vacation because of ill health. The interim manager would be coach Del Baker.

Jurges packed his bags at his hotel and said, "That's baseball. Just remember I tried as hard as I could."

Jurges went home to Washington and sent a special delivery letter to Yawkey. It began:

> DEAR MR. YAWKEY,
>
> You have been wonderful to me. There was a job to be done and I tried to do it. I really wanted to be the manager of the Red Sox. I would be glad to come back with certain provisos. . . .

The provisos, whatever they may have been, were never made public.

Jurges' rest period was terminated with the announcement that a new manager had been appointed. His name:

Michael "Pinky" Higgins.

The Red Sox finished seventh in 1960.

People said Jurges lost his job in spring training. He wasn't firm enough. Two unidentified players were in an automobile accident long after curfew. They were favored, however, and never fined. The worst slap was just the in-league joke: "That Keough can't even hit a curve with an automobile."

People remembered that at least Joe Cronin had been tough. He had playboys, but when Jim Tabor gave him trouble in training camp he both fined and suspended him, making outfielder Lou Finney the third baseman. People also remembered Finney getting hit repeatedly by ground balls and saying, "The only one being hurt by Tabor's suspension is me."

The season ground to a close, its sole saving grace Williams' home run performance in his final at bat.

On September 30, 1960, the final phase of another palace plot was completed. Yawkey fired Harris as general manager and Johnny Murphy as farm director, Murphy taking himself off to New York with a six-thumb glove to find some talent for the Mets. Higgins was appointed manager and director of player personnel and O'Connell was installed as executive vice-president. Neil Mahoney, who would discover much of the talent of 1967, became farm system director and Johnny Pesky—on the advice of Ralph Houk to Yawkey—was made manager of the Seattle farm club.

The final membership in the country club was formed. Higgins, often tired—or was it "pleurisy"?—was seen to catch catnaps in the dugout. Jensen returned to try briefly, then jumped the team in Cleveland, quitting baseball for good. Writer Harold Kaese penned an epitaph for the troubled outfielder and the Red Sox in one stroke:

"One outfielder made news by hitting four home runs in a game, another by jumping his club. Guess which one plays for the Red Sox?"

Willie Mays had hit four homers for the Giants against the Braves that day.

The season of 1961 was only distinguished by Roger Maris breaking Ruth's record by hitting his 61st home run off the pitching of the Red Sox' Tracy Stallard.

Carl Yastrzemski came up as a rookie, hit .261 and was introduced to a different kind of baseball. If anyone had an impossible dream it was only that the Red Sox make it to the first division. They finished sixth.

In 1962, the Red Sox finished eighth, distinguishing themselves only in late July when Pumpsie Green and Gene Conley attempted to fly to Bethlehem. In a long history of club jumping this was the most hilarious. Conley was the Red Sox winningest pitcher with a record of 9-and-10 (which tells you something about this team). Green was now just a utility infielder. At Yankee Stadium on July 27—isn't it always at Yankee Stadium with this team?—Conley was knocked from the mound in the third inning, an eight-run Yankee inning during which Boston committed four errors. It provided Conley with a record of pitching 21⅔ innings without his teammates scoring a run. As the team bus stopped in traffic nudging toward Newark Airport, Conley and Green departed to use a handy facility. The bus waited 15 minutes and they didn't return. Two days later Green showed up in Washington, "too sick" to play in that day's doubleheader. This was probably a wise decision anyway. Boston lost both games, 11-2 and 14-1. Higgins returned to the hotel and fined Green $1,000. Conley never did turn up until Monday. After failing to board an El Al plane for Israel due to a lack of passport, he went home to his family. When he showed up, he was fined $2,000. What happened? Why did he do it?

"Ah," he shrugged, "I guess I thought they had weaker hitters in Israel."

But it was a beautiful country club. The saga of the Red Sox was dotted with some of the wildest episodes in the history of a sport which has not confined itself to blithe spirits. Its rugged individualists were known far and wide for their ability to contribute to any party, no matter how impromptu, and they were much sought after, winning such awards as "Man of the Year" (from United Airline Stewardesses) and "Customer of the Year" (from United Liquors). Baseball was a beautiful game. The money was nice, the hours were good, and there was no pressure. Oh, maybe just a little tinge of it at the top where there was some worry about falling attendance. Perhaps just a wee small smidgeon at the base of their pride where people laughed when they heard the very name, Red Sox. But you can't have everything. Possibly, you had to have this in order to have 1967. Underneath it all there was a feeling developing. There were a few people *who cared*. But only a few.

Higgins, having done his bit afield, retired on that sparkling effort of 1962 and the Red Sox—needing running room, requiring some kind of better press—sought their next sacrificial lamb in honest Johnny Pesky, the shortstop who hung onto the ball in the 1946 World Series.

Pesky had done an excellent job at Seattle (although some thought he should never have sent Radatz up). Pesky got the word he would be the manager from guess who? Ralph Houk. Figures. Houk suggested he stop by Tom Yawkey's suite in New York.

Pesky said later:

"I opened the door and Mr. Yawkey said, 'Have a drink. How do you like baseball? How would you like to manage the Red Sox?'

"I was the manager. Just like that."

It was the worst thing that ever happened to Pesky, who fought his way up from the bottom, up from being a shoeshine boy for Bobby Doerr in the Portland, Oregon, clubhouse before the war. He was a gay, honest little man, affectionately called "Needlenose," the result of a Cyranoic protrusion, and a friend to all. He admired Cronin and McCarthy most of all the managers he had known, regaled friends with a story about Cronin and a pitcher who did not do well, the pitcher sweating it out as they showered, dressed and enplaned for the next town, Cronin never saying a word and then, when the plane was airborne, stating: "When we get to 10,000 feet, jump out."

Baseball, as you may be discovering, is not always a funny game. For Pesky it was sheer tragedy. He tried to command and was defeated by Higgins and Yastrzemski. The makings of the 1967 team were there. Indeed, as an historical note in 1963 and 1964, one of the players would be Dick Williams and the other would be Eddie Bressoud, who went over to the Cardinals.

Pesky thought the game was for real. Everyone else thought it was permanently spring training. Higgins signed Richard "the King" Stuart, a first baseman of such dubious merit that he enjoyed describing his fielding efforts in this fashion:

"Once I bent down to pick up a gum wrapper and I got a standing ovation."

Stuart, a man of monumental ego, could hit, however, which was more than you could say for most of the Red Sox. A near-miss superstar, he was still such a name on this slumping and inept team that he was given his own television show, which he distinguished with such opening remarks as:

"Hello, this is the Dick Stuart Show. Welcome to the Dick Stuart Show, Larry. This is the first time you've been on the Dick Stuart Show, isn't it?"

Stuart also distinguished himself by consistently undermining Pesky's authority and by a wild clubhouse fight with Earl Wilson, who had finally made it to the team (the old Negro policies were no longer in force). Yaz even won a batting championship in 1963. But the Red Sox finished seventh and they had a good alibi. In spring training, Pesky had worked them too hard. He drilled on fundamentals and even had the pitchers practice sliding. As late as July 15, the Red

Sox were actually up in the ozone, baby, way up there, baby, in second place, only five and a half games behind the Yankees. Then they just got tired.

Or quit.

Pesky came to Boston full of bounce, with statements like, "I love people, but this is no popularity contest. I'm no louse, but I can be one if I have to be."

His weakness in 1963 was tipping his coaches off on curfews—infrequently called—and not slamming down on offenders. But he couldn't anyway, because no matter what happened the real manager of the team sat up in Higgins' office.

Yastrzemski admits today that there were times in this period when he did not exactly extend himself. One night, in Boston, Gary Peters was scheduled to pitch for the White Sox, a southpaw tough on left-handed hitters like Yaz, who conveniently developed a stomachache and could not play. Later that night, Pesky dropped into a fried chicken place near the park and found Yaz devouring a plate of chicken, onion rings and French fries. Pesky's attempts at disciplining him only caused Pesky trouble in the front office.

He was in a vacuum, a weird vacuum where the players controlled the team, where you couldn't punch back from the top. There was something called the Radatz Ratpack. Radatz, a huge man called "the Monster," blazed his fast ball for three years and gained the reputation of being the greatest modern "fireman" of them all, at the same time coining such phrases as "Wait until I get my six-pack of V.O. and I'll be right there" and, after a player meeting, "We're not going to drink any more this year. Of course, we're not going to drink any less, either."

His huge muscles rippling, he and Yaz and Stuart were the only things Boston could even remotely be pleased about, and the Monster strutted in daily from the bullpen until

1965 when his demise into Frankenstein was sudden. The fastball was gone and so was Radatz.

But Pesky had it in these years, the years of the Ratpack—perhaps none as rich as Sinatra's group, but living in much the same style; laughing, *living*, baby, *living* and, of course, losing.

Pesky never was the choice of Higgins. Higgins had wanted Herman, who you will recall was assigned first with Jurges and with Hig. But Yawkey had selected Pesky and the two seasons, 1963 and 1964, had to be endured. The first was a horror. The second was worse.

Days of wine and roses and days, as well, of screaming matches, players who wouldn't play, wouldn't train, wouldn't sleep, either, it seemed to the casual observer.

By 1964, another important part of the impossible dream of 1967 had enlisted. Tony Conigliaro. It was questionable whether he signed with the Ratpack or the Red Sox. Looking back on it, Tony said:

"I didn't do anything any other kid would do under the same circumstances," which may be a fairly accurate answer to the continual question of this period—What is the matter with the Red Sox?

By June, Pesky was convinced he should quit, which he nearly did after Stuart let a couple of balls go through his legs. "There were a lot of things before that, too," Pesky said. "I benched him in Kansas City for not trying. So he comes up to me on the bench and this is how it went:

STUART: "John, why am I not playing?"

PESKY: "After the way you played last night how can you ask me that?"

STUART: "John, I'm just three or four RBIs from being the RBI king of this league."

PESKY: "I'm just interested in winning baseball games."

STUART: "John, you just like me as a person—not as a ballplayer."

PESKY: "You said it, I didn't."

STUART: "John, you just don't care about RBIs and home runs because you didn't get many yourself."

In telling the story, Pesky shrugged, laughed, with a tinge it seemed of bitterness. The story is a perfect answer to the question of what *was* wrong with the Red Sox.

The best results stemmed from Pesky's determination to stick it out; from the fact that Dick Williams as a player was learning what really was wrong with the Red Sox and from the fact that Yawkey himself was getting a little bored with being too patient, too good a guy.

But Pesky was foredoomed. During the winter Yastrzemski had even gone so far as to publicly degrade him in a speech. No action was taken.

By July, he was issuing fines, a $250 one to Conigliaro for a curfew violation, the fine coming just before Conigliaro—logy and unable to get out of the way—was hit by a pitch and broke his forearm.

By August Pesky was saying, "I can't stand it. It's a nightmare. Maybe somebody should take a poke at somebody."

By September it was very obvious that he most certainly would be gone. Yawkey left for his Carolina plantation. A press conference was announced for Friday. Pesky was not invited, but he grimly stuck it out, managing the team in the dugout while his executioners watched from above.

At 9 A.M. Friday, Higgins had breakfast with Pesky and said, "We've decided to make a change."

Another episode in the Frank Merriwellian chapter of the Red Sox was over. They had sortied determinedly into eighth place. The new manager would be the man Higgins wanted long, long ago. Jurges' old double play mate, Pesky's coach—Billy Herman.

Sound of drums. Ruffles and flourishes. We'll win more than we lose. First division here we come.

They were ninth—a good, solid, undistinguished ninth—in both 1965 and 1966 and Herman now had a taste of what it was like to try to put some life into a team which had no interest.

His two years would lead to the dream of 1967. He, too, would be a sacrificial lamb. There was no other way now. Baseball had fallen onto the times of CBS. The "New Breed" was different, in gray flannel knickers or gray flannel suits. The old coaches, players and general managers, and the old ideas, were going.

If they left behind them an equal legacy of greatness and greed, then that was just the way sport was. Each manager who left the Red Sox always said that Yawkey was a good man, that there were many good players on the team. But there were also the others.

Now in these next two years, Herman would attempt to make baseball players out of Conigliaro, Petrocelli, and Yastrzemski, and to weed out those who had to go. Meanwhile, Mahoney had built up a farm system which was working for a change, and O'Connell was becoming a modern major league executive. Higgins—the last veteran of the palace guard which had caused so many coups—would have to go. They entered 1965, each man knowing the facts, Yawkey determined that he was going to rebuild this team. Dick Williams was through as a player, sent to Toronto to try his hand at managing and take a couple of years away from the Ratpack, meanwhile to get to know the rest of the young talent which would be coming up, Foy, Andrews, Smith.

Meanwhile, they took their lumps. Herman took the hardest ones. He went through 1965 with a ragtag assortment of dispirited players. Radatz no longer led any charge. In the honored fashion of frustrated fans, the Monster who was cheered each time he strutted in to relieve was booed as soon as he made an appearance. The Red Sox lost 100 games in 1965, the low-water mark of their careers. Stuart was traded. The old gangs were breaking up. Yawkey paternalized, cajoled, fined—and this time made the fines stick. The rumblings underneath were not visible on the surface. It was still a lousy club. Everyone *knew* that. The country club. At times, it lived up to its reputation. Conigliaro lived up to their brilliant social reputation and was slapped down for it, really slapped with a $1,000 fine which stuck. Even his teammates had enough of that stuff. They blew the whistle on him in the press when Herman caught a slew of them out after curfew and Conigliaro copped a plea with the press:

"I wasn't one of them. May my head fall off my shoulders if I was."

His head rolled with the team and the front office. From this point on there was the unique possibility that he just might become a good professional baseball player.

Haywood Sullivan, the catcher whose name Higgins couldn't remember, became the manager of the Kansas City Athletics—the Kansas City Athletics?—while in transit back to Boston.

On September 17, 1965, the final, most difficult stroke of the renaissance of the Red Sox took place.

Yawkey fired Higgins and made Dick O'Connell general manager.

It began in the morning. Higgins told Yawkey, "Look, I'm not popular around here. You better get a new man."

Yawkey replied, "Okay. We'll make the change after the World Series."

Then, as they sat watching from their rooftop box, Yawkey changed his mind and said, "I guess I'd like to make the change now." The announcement was prepared for release after the game.

It figured the way Red Sox history runs that the announcement would be made under unusual circumstances. Their pitcher, Dave Morehead, threw a no-hitter against the Indians that day, but Yawkey went ahead with the decision anyway.

Higgins said in parting, "The next general manager you get better fit in with the front office," which seemed like a fitting farewell from the last expert of the palace guard. He added, "Don't be too hard on Yawkey. He and I have been friends for a long time."

Down on the field, as Morehead prepared to throw his final pitch to Davalillo, he chanced to ask Bressoud—the man who would next face Boston as a Cardinal—what to throw. "Do it on your own," Bressoud said. "If you don't you'll eat your heart out for the rest of your life." The no-hitter went into the record books and in the ways strange to baseball it naturally was a second story to the main event—HIGGINS FIRED. Someone told Morehead not to feel badly, reminding him that the day Gehrig hit four home runs it was the second story to the news that McGraw had quit the Giants.

Yawkey said his decision was the toughest he ever had to make. But this was a new, tough Yawkey.

In New Brunswick, where he was fishing, Ted Williams let it be known that he would accept the general manager's job if Yawkey asked him. But the job was already O'Connell's. Ted remained fishing.

At the winter meetings in Fort Lauderdale, the timing was more perfect. Promptly at 4 P.M., on November 29, 1965, Haywood Sullivan emerged in one wing of the hotel to be announced as the vice-president of player personnel of the Red Sox, while in the other wing Alvin Dark, who had been waiting in the wings, stepped forward to be announced as Sullivan's replacement to manage the Kansas City Athletics, a job he would retain until 1967 when the Finley-Harrelson-Krausse incident would end his connection.

Baseball is a daffy game.

Musical chairs, played against a backdrop of green diamonds, bright floodlights, crowds around the beer counter and front office executives around a bar.

And wisecracks:

"Haywood Sullivan? Which paper clips will he be in charge of?"

"This is the craziest thing that's happened since the night the sea gull dropped the fish on the mound while Ellis Kinder was pitching."

"I'm not surprised. If the Red Sox finished ninth, then naturally they'd go to a tenth-place manager for their brains."

"I don't know what Haywood Sullivan can do for them, but if they brought back Frank Sullivan they'd at least lead the league in wisecracks."

The comment was unkind, but it was a comment based on a long history of yesterday's promises, of almost-pennants and never-weres. No one except the very few on the inside knew that there was a change coming at last. It was subtle. But it was there. The country club of baseball was ceasing membership applications. The worst team in baseball—and indeed it was the worst team in baseball, because at least the Mets tried—was going to take a new shot for it.

They would make mistakes, such as trading Earl Wilson, who had pitched a no-hitter in 1962—and who would come back to haunt them in 1967. But at least they were more honest mistakes than some of the trades in the past.

Meanwhile, Herman still had to be the goat. The law of sacrifice demanded it. Herman and Maglie were the final hangovers from the old days. Dick Williams still needed more experience and was only one of several under consideration. Mele was in trouble with Griffith and he might make a very logical Boston manager, back in his hometown, back where he had begun as a player.

Underneath it all, you could just feel the slightest touch of it, of the beginning of a hardening and a formation of something better. They had let down some fine players, men like

Frank Malzone, who gallantly squandered their talents on a team of complete ineptitude. Now it was time to re-create substance from squalor.

Herman was doing it the best way he could. He still faced some of the spoiled kids who ran to the front office. In 1965 he was forced to undergo the silliness of a summit meeting with Tony Conigliaro and his father, Sal, while people asked, "Would Ralph Houk do that?" This wasn't Ralph Houk's team, even though he helped to appoint some of the managers. It was Yawkey's team now, and O'Connell's and Sullivan's, and if these pages have been critical of them on the one hand, then they deserve some credit in 1965 and 1966 as they kept a tight rein, kept their mouths reasonably shut under the barrage of criticism of two straight ninth-place finishes, and made their plans.

Herman opened spring training with a rigged election for a team captain. The captain would have to be a regular, he insisted. Since only Yastrzemski and Conigliaro were regulars it was obvious that Yaz would be the captain. The tradition of the Ratpack was slowly being broken up. Yastrzemski was a very poor captain, caught between his playmates and his manager, and still far from an inspirational leader. It was the last low blow which he had to suffer for his own inadequacies. Yastrzemski hated being the captain. "I had my own problems," he remembered. "I got the feeling the guys were giving me the cold shoulder. Everytime someone had a gripe they came to me. I was arguing on behalf of guys like Conigliaro for missing curfew, saying it was a mistake, and then finding out I had been lied to. I hated it. I had to do some deep thinking about this whole thing with the Red Sox and about myself."

Herman had his hands full with Petrocelli, the moody kid who would become an impresario at shortstop, but who was still playing it in 1966 with the temperament of an operatic soprano.

In spring training, there were some lucky breaks. George Scott came along. On the afternoon of March 30—by one of those sheerest of chances common to baseball—the Cardinals' Red Schoendienst wanted to test a left-handed pitcher he might be using in relief. Dalton Jones was scheduled to bat against a right-hander. Schoendienst called for the southpaw. "I even made a little wave at Herman just to let him know I wasn't trying anything smart," Schoendienst remembered later. "Hell, this wasn't the World Series. I just wanted to see if the lefty could pitch."

Herman didn't see the hand wave. But he did react to the change and called Jones back and looked down his bench for a right-handed hitter. The decision had been privately made to send Scott to Toronto and go with Joe Foy, who was playing a much better third base, but Scotty was an anxious kid. Anytime there was a chance that a right-handed batter might be needed as a pinch hitter, Scott would pick up a bat and start loosening up. His movement caught Herman's eye.

"Go up and hit, Scotty."

To some it was only a spring training game. To George Scott it was everything in his life: security for his family; staying in the big league. He hit a line smash which went over the fence in center and seemed to keep right on going.

Scott, with an assist from Schoendienst, was on the Red Sox to stay, becoming a first baseman and in this season of 1966 winning the job of the All Star first baseman of the American League.

Of such small things is baseball also made. Now the luck, the breaks, were going with the Red Sox.

By June, the Red Sox were still floundering. Wilson was traded to Detroit and Maglie was saying, "Wilson is only a .500 pitcher."

Wilson replied, "Well, they weren't even a .500 team." Wilson's efforts at Detroit bore out the error of the trade. Yawkey exploded again about a poor press, but what else could it be, and Herman foxed his way along trying to get something other than average baseball out of Conigliaro, Yastrzemski and Petrocelli, saying at the same time, "If I lose my job, it will be because of Petrocelli."

His job was already lost. A decision had to be made about the future of Dick Williams, who was receiving offers in Toronto and, besides, in the game of front office baseball there is no room for the manager who is labeled as an appointee of the general manager who went before.

The newspapers compared O'Connell, Sullivan and Herman to the Three Musketeers—Athos, Porthos, and Aramis. They were everywhere together and seemingly hit it off beautifully. It is always good to be friendly with the doomed man, to ease his last gallows walk. Yawkey had begun making the decision in May when Yastrzemski called a team meeting in California. The Red Sox lost five straight and "Captain Yaz" (this was not in his Captain Marvel days) called the meeting to tell the players to "relax." They relaxed so well they made it six straight losses and after that Herman—who had always harbored the desire—was outspoken in his hopes to trade Yastrzemski.

But you don't trade that kind of man when you are trying to build a pennant winner. The weakening Herman was getting another bad mark from the First Team in the front office.

Yet Herman was still a really good baseball man. He started Scott at third base, replacing Foy, even though Foy had been voted Minor League Player of the Year in 1965. As the Red Sox continued to slump toward ninth, Herman made the decision to bring Foy back at third and make a first baseman out of Scott. Scotty didn't like playing on the other side of the infield for the first time. But it was the *big* league and the only way to stay was to become a first baseman . . . and then to become the best one in the league, and he did. Herman helped.

It may not have appeared so at the time, but he was helping with Lonborg and Brandon as well, forcing them, sitting them in the bullpen for extended periods, teaching them.

In the second half of the season—far too late to do any good, but enough to begin to jell—the Red Sox were the equal of any team on the American League fields. They were winning and a few were even seen to be showing some real pride in their work.

The Boston press did not attack Herman. At least, *they* knew he was a baseball man. It was working out. Some of them even told off players like Yaz; telling them off because "even if I am a friend of yours it's time you knew the truth about yourself and this team." Add an assist to the Boston press.

In early September, the Red Sox came in from a road trip and Yaz was saying, "Next year, I'm not going to be a politician. I'm going to be a player."

The decision came too late for Herman. He came in to pick up his mail. It was September 9, 1966. The Orioles were striking toward the American League pennant. The Red Sox were in ninth place, but coming off an 8-6 road trip and playing better. Herman stopped by O'Connell's office. They talked for two minutes, at the end of which Herman was fired. He asked to see Yawkey, but the owner was unavailable, attending a Jimmy Fund function. He asked to see Sullivan and all three men sat in the front office, chatting. Yawkey would give a 100 percent recommendation, Herman was told. But he was still fired.

Herman asked, "Why?"

Neither of the other two men attempted to answer. The answer lay somewhere far back, perhaps all the way back to the beginning. But it was too deep a reason. It was the rule of baseball. The change would be made. A press conference was called and the writers straggled to Fenway, confident that the conference would only be a routine announcement that Herman was being reappointed for another season.

O'Connell—the New Breed executive, the man who survived it all and learned from it and was capable at it—said:

"It pains me to say this. But the Red Sox have decided to make a change . . ."

Pete Runnels, the soft-spoken Texan who won two batting titles with the Red Sox and was now a coach, took over the team for the remainder of the year. On September 28, Dick Williams was officially announced as the new manager. His contract would be for just one year. There was talk of first division. It sounded like the same old battle cry, the same old Klaxon ringing to call in the season ticket customers. No one realized it at the time, but the race for the impossible dream was on. Writers said, "The next Red Sox manager should be a strong man—a very strong man, strong enough to run the whole show without interference, strong enough to handle the officials, the players and the sportswriters as well." (One wag added, "If they find a man like this they should run him for President.")

In Pompano Beach, Florida, Herman was saying:

"I never knew Tom Yawkey well, but in the last months of the season he began calling me to his office and we spent quite a bit of time chatting. I thought we were getting along. I can't fault him, though. He was good to me."

Herman shifted to the Angels as a coach. The new man was Williams the Second, the man nobody was going to push around, the man who would have to make it all come true in one year.

If the Red Sox were a 100-to-1 shot, then he was a 1,000-to-1 shot. Everyone *knew* that. Red Sox managers never last. They aren't tough enough.

Oh yeah?

Watch this one. As they say, he was a beautiful thing to watch in action—even when he blew some.

7.

Williams the Second

HE WAS a man with fine and dandy in his eyes and perhaps a drop of ice water in his heart. He was signed to just a one-year contract and yet he had the cheek to take a two-year lease on his apartment and buy his furniture on three-year terms.

Maybe that will tell you something about baseball. The thing he wanted more than anything else was enough money to own his home. The thing, the inescapable, unphrasable thing he had going for him was a cocksure knowledge that he might just be able to pull it off and, what-the-hell, if he didn't then he at least was at last getting his chance up there, up in the big league.

Long beyond the season, long beyond the record books which will coldly indicate the statistics of who did what under which pressures—long beyond all of this, there will be guys for years standing in bars with a beer or cooling a gin and tonic on the veranda of a country club remembering back to the one year when Williams pulled it off.

For this was his team. To make or break. At the blowoff, at the very end, there would still be some players who hated him, there were others who didn't like him and there were some who thought he was a brilliant manager, but one they couldn't get close to.

After this season, he would be faced with a minor uprising from young Conigliaro, who speaking at a dinner on Boston's North Shore—shades of Yaz' speech about Pesky only a few years before—would tear into Williams, saying:

"Williams deserves a lot of credit. But everyone is forgetting the players who did the work. All the credit is going to the manager and the players aren't getting their share. I don't mean just Yastrzemski, Lonborg and the stars. I mean all the guys, like Dalton Jones, Mike Ryan, George Thomas, Elston Howard. All the credit is going to Williams when it was a team effort.

"Joe Foy was treated wrongly," Conigliaro added. "Joe was making mistakes, but he wasn't handled right. Some guys need a pat on the back, others need to be handled more firmly. I personally want someone to yell at me and Foy is the same way."

Conigliaro—who was wound up and couldn't untrack—added such other pungent comments as: "Foy should play regularly next season and George Scott should be kept on first base. Dalton Jones is strictly a hitter. If he played regularly, he could hurt you more over a year than he could help you."

Later, Conigliaro, about to leave for a fifteen-day trip to Vietnam, insisted the Jones remark was misunderstood, that it was said only in reference to a comparison to having Foy on third base. He did not recant the other statements.

In Florida, Williams maintained a silence, which was smarter than statements some other managers made; and Conigliaro—who earlier in his career had dodged doing his required Army Reserve service (he did not rejoin an active Reserve unit after his military service at Fort Dix) and who had just gotten back in under the wire of being recalled for eighteen months of active duty by the Pentagon—flew off to Vietnam. Conigliaro, whose ego always seemed to get him in trouble, as the reader will remember from the last chapter, deserved at least credit for the job he did in Vietnam, although fifteen days is not a military combat career, and Joe DiMaggio, his traveling mate there, may have summed it up best when he said:

"Tony is a very nice kid. He talks a lot about girls, though."

Williams deserved credit for not blowing his stack. But this was one more insight into the domain of Williams the Second—the one Williams who made this team finally a winner.

He came to Boston on the basis of two straight Little World Series victories with Toronto in 1965 and 1966, after he ended a thirteen-year major league career with the Sox in 1964, a member of the country club team, but one of the few members who did not like the conditions of membership. That Williams hung on for thirteen years in the majors was in itself a tribute to the inner man; this thirty-eight-year-old man who would make his mistakes, but who would still be on top of it all at the end, understanding his game, understanding the men, the front office, the hidden ground rules which had destroyed so many others before him.

His career was shortened right at the outset when he made a good play in the outfield of the Brooklyn Dodgers as they were charging toward a pennant—and why shouldn't the one manager who finally straightened out the Red Sox come from the old, wild Dodgers and have been born in St. Louis? Even that figured.

It was early in the year and he charged a ball, catching it, falling, rolling and feeling something pop and still getting up and throwing the ball in toward a runner. The rest of his career was second-rate from that point and, indeed, he would sit in the press box during that World Series of 1956, which the Yankees won in seven—get the number, seven, a natural with this Williams—and would sit there knowing that he had only been cut in for a one-third share of the

World Series jackpot by his teammates; cut out because he was injured early.

His greatest value throughout a journey across five teams and innumerable apartments and suitcases was that he was a great sign stealer (perhaps this ability with the 1967 Red Sox will never be told) and an even greater bench jockey, a rhubarb, bossy, cocky kind of guy whom a manager could afford to carry as a utility outfielder, because if nothing else he added an élan, a sense of being *in there,* of actually being part of *it* even in the depths of a dugout.

He did it all, and if sometimes the words were harsh and if there are those who will make judgments of him privately that they would not to his face, then this, too, is part of what made up the impossible year, the pursuit of this 100-to-1 shot which no one would really, *not really,* risk a bet on.

Dick Williams was just one more in a long succession of last-place Red Sox managers. Everyone *knew* that. He was only given a one-year contract because the Red Sox had every intention of dumping him and signing up a local man, Sam Mele, if things didn't work out right with Griffith's Twins. Everyone knew that, too. Boston blew one good manager in its minor league system, Gene Mauch, who was permitted to go over into the National League—the National League, for God's sakes, I mean, how could this be allowed to happen?—and Boston couldn't take the chance on another insult like that. So they would bring this cocky Williams up and he would fall on his kisser and that would be an end to *that.*

Which may be the very reason for his success. Because he knew it, too.

He was stuck with some things he didn't like. Sal Maglie was carried over as a pitching coach. Maglie was Billy Herman's boy, but the salary—the $20,000 salary—was too much to settle up for and by odd circumstance, Maglie, an old Brooklyn teammate, had to be carried.

The only way to handle Maglie was to cut him out. Williams did just that, applying a harsh rule of baseball. When Maglie was let go at the end of the season there were reverberations. Maglie, whose nickname "the Barber" came from close shaves at the plate more than from his adeptness with a razor, had an unfortunate year, losing his wife suddenly and tragically and then, after being fired (or, more reasonably in that strange maze of the front office, "not having his option picked up"), was involved in an automobile accident in Buffalo which hospitalized him, his neck in traction.

By this time, Williams was already the Manager of the Year and Conigliaro had already popped off.

Williams—one eye still on Mele, who was now gone from the Twins and a Fenway Park fixture, a confidant of the mighty, a man waiting for a new assignment—had nevertheless forced through a three-year contract at $55,000 per, plus extras, the best contract Yawkey had given since the days of Cronin. (It was said, privately, that Yawkey was pleased with Williams, but hurt, as well, because Williams, the pennant winner, the man who carried them to seven games, would not settle for just two years. No, Williams knew the rules of this game. He wanted the security of three years and he got it; getting as well the new house in Florida, the concrete and the stucco poured to his precise measurement, and let's all enjoy it and think about it because it is good in this world to see one man able at least to get the things he has set his heart on; to not back up and take one year or two, but to go for the whole score, the whole $165,000, plus fringe benefits which went with the impossible dream.)

Williams could have ducked this one. Maglie was tired, unhappy and out of it. A good guy, a great pitcher, a man who gave up a lifetime job for the State of New York to venture back into the maelstrom of big league politics, an ex-teammate and a man stung by being left completely out of

Cocky Dick Williams had a word for a bystander.

Williams meets with Cronin during 1967 World Series.

Williams the First, typically with bat in hand, has an intent discussion with Williams the Second before leaving spring training in 1967.

Left **The taste of victory for Williams as Red Sox tied series at three games each.**

Right **Dick Williams was a good utility player with the Red Sox for two years before leaving to manage Toronto.**

everything; just a stranger sitting amidst men who suddenly had the fever of winning *it*.

So Maglie sounded off as well and his statements must therefore be recorded and considered, for if we are to know what made all of this possible, then we must know the past history and the present and the inside of what really went on as they came down the stretch in the Great Race, the great, floundering race where no one could give it away and everyone had to finally fight it out to the last dramatic weekend.

Maglie was bitterly angry. One of the finest pitchers of his era, he was replaced on the Red Sox by a catcher, Darrell Johnson, a man who caught only 134 games during an eleven-year span.

Johnson was a friend from Dick's own playing days in Baltimore and a rival manager (Baltimore's Rochester franchise) in the International League. "Old friends and old rivals, a man I know can do the job," Williams said on hiring him.

Two days later, Maglie fired back; tired, hospitalized, alone and doing the one thing that automatically disqualifies a man forever from the big league: talking from the heart. Maglie knew when he said it that his days were over and one must respect him for that. The unwritten rules of baseball are stronger than the Ten Commandments. Cry "Cop!" and step permanently outside.

But from his hospital bed, Maglie told Boston columnist George Sullivan by telephone:

"I got a lousy deal from Williams. I'm not going to keep quiet for a guy like that. I'm well rid of Williams and those around him. It made me sick to see what was going on among them. Who are them? I don't care to say. Just leave it at that. They'll know who I mean. I want to make it clear I'm not talking about the front office. . . . They were wonderful to me and I'm grateful. I'm not happy leaving the organization, but I'm well rid of *them*. I had a miserable season. I wouldn't go through it again. I'm telling the truth, not sneaking around like Williams. The guy never listened to me and he only gave sarcastic answers.

"He didn't listen to me in the seventh game of the World Series. It was obvious Lonborg didn't have it. Williams should have gotten him out of there earlier and I told him so. It was a crime that he let a man who'd done such a great job for him all season take a pounding like that. It was degrading.

"Naturally, Lonborg didn't ask to be taken out. What was he supposed to say: 'Take me out'? But I'm sure Lonnie would have been happier out of there much earlier. He knew as well as we did how tired he was and how much it affected him.

"What's more we still had a chance to win. I'm not second-guessing Williams. I'm just stating the facts and the obvious.

"So Williams didn't listen to my advice, but as I've said, that was nothing new. It got so frustrating during the season that I just shut up. But then I thought again. I knew I was getting paid to speak up and I did. That's what I get paid for. But it didn't do any good. All I got was sarcasm or a deaf ear.

"And that's when he talked to me at all.

"After the Series, he said: 'I'll be talking to you.'

"I'm still waiting. He never had the courage or the decency to tell me I was fired.

"Look, I'm no fool. I know he wouldn't have had me there except that I had a year on my contract. I went to him during the season and offered to step aside, to quit.

"He didn't have the courage to take me up on it and he didn't have the courage to tell me when I was through. Then he turns around and tells people that he didn't agree with my methods of handling pitchers. He had these other guys in mind all the way along.

"I'll tell you one thing, though. The Red Sox have some serious pitching problems ahead—they desperately need two pitchers and one of them a left-hander.

"Williams may be the toast of the town now, but I've seen people hit the popularity skids before and I'll see it happen fast again."

Maglie hung up. In anger and fury.

In Florida—living in just one more apartment waiting for that new home to go up—Williams answered:

"I have great respect for Sal Maglie as a pitcher and a gentleman. But I made a decision and he had to go. I told Dick O'Connell and asked if I should call him. Dick said he would. But Sal is right. I should have called the man. I told him I would."

The answer provided a finesse which only all the years could have provided. Williams is shrewd. A *smart* baseball man. Other men might have salvoed right back, especially dealing from the top of a deck loaded with a pennant, an MVP, a Cy Young Award winner and a front office which had O'Connell as the Executive of the Year. And Williams, of course, as Manager of the Year. That he did not, that he managed his way through this as well, is one more indication of Williams, the man.

Williams is the new kind of manager. This writer holds no brief for him, one way or the other, for it is not the purpose of this book to enshrine anyone. Nor is it my purpose to defame anyone. They are all men doing the best they can, during a period now—as we approach these last chapters—of the greatest turmoil in the history of our nation. The Casey Stengels and the Joe McCarthys are gone. The Joe Cronins have moved from stage center. The Ted Williamses have gone fishing.

The tough utility men, who know all the knocks, are coming along.

Maglie, even before his final salvo, his final blast from a hospital ("Sad, sad," people in the league front offices called it, not recognizing it for what it was; courageous, defiant and the end of an era, the passing of the banner on to the frontrunners of another period), Maglie had said something even before, near the end of the Series.

"What does Williams want?" he asked. "What does he mean, teach? What is this, a minor league or something? What does a pitcher have to know besides throwing the ball over the plate hard and with something on it? What is this teach?"

The valedictory in itself is sad.

The years have come when men must do more. Williams cut Maglie out early because he recognized a holdover threat—another possible palace revolt—and more than that the singular fact that pitchers are now more human. Alexander may have been as great drunk as sober and Kinder may have been the finest Old Granddad of them all, but this is the time now of the Thinking Man's pitcher. Koufax is gone, but he left his own legacy, one to give succor and understanding to such as Lonborg. The days of the old coaches are gone now as well. There are coaches who must have the trust of their young flock, but the key is the trust between player and manager and the knowledge that player and manager must have that this is a 52-week game; a game now where the result on May 1 is as important as on September 30 and a business where you get paid for what you are.

Williams relied more on his trainer, Buddy LeRoux—the same man who evolutionized professional basketball in many more ways than just taping when he was with the Celtics—and as many decisions were made by players in the training room during the season and on the telephone in the winter (what shape are you in; are you doing your exercises) as were ever made in the old days by a whole pride of coaches, sitting late into the night in managers' suites or in owners' penthouses talking about the good old days.

Yes, he was new and crusty and cocky and different, this Williams. Some of the things he did, Maglie would never understand. Some of the things Maglie accused him of were faults which were no longer applicable to the modern game; of which we will discuss more as we enter the chapters of this remarkable season and the World Series itself.

But before the season, before the Series, there was still this man, Williams, who to this moment has never been covered, delved into in depth, because like the more superb cases of any person who surfaces briefly to dominate an era, he projects a challenge which leaves anyone to question the final judgment.

He plays a tight, close hand.

He would have been the world's greatest fool if he had not.

Williams stands out. An individualist. A careful swashbuckler, who will cut a wider swath now that he has the security each man seeks.

One tries to think of how it can all be summed up. These pages are so full of baseball and of legend, but the best thing might be Williams the man and his feeling for his son, Rick, the little boy he dressed in uniform and made an auxiliary bat boy, knowing full well that there were those who would second-guess him even for this and call it "bush-league"—because it had never been done before.

Williams didn't care what *they* said and if anything he gave to the boy, Rick, a memory which few fathers can. Yet, on the Friday after the Series had ended, a scant 24 hours later, making his final definitive arrangements for his security and that of his family, he forgot his son.

It is a small, cameo scene which may tell more about the man than one ordinarily knows. In the front office there were those who said, "It's a frame-up. He shouldn't hold Mr. Yawkey up for that extra year. He'll be sorry."

Williams stuck to his demand for a three-year contract and now he had received it and the press conference would be held on Saturday. Bobby Doerr—a coach appreciated and valued—was with him as Williams left the park, the two men driving north over the Mystic River Bridge to the apartment and the furniture on a three-year payment plan, when Williams suddenly remembered something was missing.

Within the hour he was back at Fenway, picking up the son, waiting, watching as the ground crew carefully rolled up the left-field turf of which Yawkey was making a gift to Yastrzemski for a lawn at his new house.

He laughed and shook his head to think that after all of this he could forget the boy; but it had been one more day of accomplishment, of achieving one more phase of the impossible dream—achieving $165,000 and fringe benefits—and now they roared back over the bridge, and whether he is ever a Casey Stengel or a Joe McCarthy is considerably less important. He is a man. Simply. Cockily. And, usually, very wisely.

He had come a long, long way on this very day when it would also be announced that Billy Herman was no longer a coach for the California Angels and Johnny Pesky was no longer a coach for the Pirates.

There is an underlying viciousness to the game. But, for the time, Williams conquered it.

He came to spring training an unknown quotient, an X factor, and when he made his first statements there were those who recorded them and said, "Yeah. Same old ——."

He said, "We'll win more than we lose."

He believed, as did everyone, that this was just the normal statement of a second division manager. I mean, how do you ever come from last into the first division? And no one ever comes from last to first. Right? Of course. Even Williams knew that. But with a little luck, oh, just a little luck, and with that good front office team operating at last—Yawkey and O'Connell and Sullivan and Mahoney—with no problems with palace coups d'état, then perhaps they could do something.

So as we lead into this strangest of seasons, knowing some of the cast of characters, some of the country club set, it is also necessary to know the new man in town, the new deals and what happened as they began the final six months which led to this crystallized, superb moment when baseball again was something to be cherished as part of our America, a nice, good, strong part, the Walter Mitty-ish dream of every man; men who knew they could play this game as well as the Red Sox—"Hell, couldn't anyone?" they would ask, and turn off radios and televisions in disgust, more betrayed, even, than people in Kansas City, for at least they had once had the impossible in hand and had once known greatness and now it was all an absurdity. No man who watched thought he couldn't play better than *they* could. And who knows, in the stands there were men who probably could have at least tried better at that.

He took over by surprise, slipping in during an announcement which caught everyone flat-footed. He spent the winter trying his best to juggle some of his players into shape, contacting LeRoux and using him to call each man at least once a week, forcing them to at least think of being in shape.

He came to them at Winter Haven as a half-stranger, a fellow player two seasons removed into the high minors, a man respected by Smith, Foy, Andrews, Scott, Ryan, and Gibson, who played for him at Toronto. A man questioned by Yastrzemski and Conigliaro. Just another manager to the more erudite Lonborg, whose counsel was always his own. A guy passing through to some of the sportswriting cliques who (1) adored Higgins; (2) adored Herman; (3) knew for a fact that nothing was going to happen, anyway, and who accepted what had once been a fine assignment as just another tedious embarkation on a long season of plane rides and press rooms.

He came as a man to be watched by the front office. He would *never* make it, of course. But he might serve a purpose. He might *just* break up the old mob. For the front office knew what it was doing. At long last they knew. A couple of years and they would have a good manager and a contender.

The Red Sox heard a lot of stories about him. A player in Toronto whacked him in the mouth one day, knocking him to his knees. (Later, Dennis Bennett would threaten to "go Mencke one better" and knock him out and disappear shortly thereafter.)

Bob Cerv, a former good ballplayer, would make a statement: "I don't know about his all-for-one attitude. All I can think of is the year we were fighting for the club RBI championship at Kansas City. It was late in the season—Dick was on second base with two out—and I hit a single to right. When I looked up, there was Dick Williams trotting into third."

He had Doerr now as a coach—a decent, honorable man who could get along with anyone; a man who would never carry a tale. Doerr in his own way might have settled Williams down here and there.

Williams brought Al Lakeman back to the majors as his bullpen coach, bringing him back to the same team which he had left after the Pesky "problem."

And he had this little fellow, Eddie Popowski, up to the majors for his very first time, coaching at last after all those years shepherding kids through the low minors. Popowski was brought up really for one reason—to handle the volatile Petrocelli, who had caused Herman to be fired and who, after two long winter talks with Yawkey, still needed gentle handling. The theory with Petrocelli, as applied by Popowski, was never to boost him when he was going well, because he had a built-in mistrust of front-runner applause.

And he had Maglie, the problem, one which would have to be more gently solved.

There are few things really gentle about Dick Williams. But he would survive as a unique ambassador in the United Nations—or in Saigon.

This was his game and his deal. One game, one deal for the jackpot.

He began it with the early conditioning and with scales which were no longer fixed to hide overweight. There had been the careful off-season trades by O'Connell and Sullivan. There was the increased interest of Yawkey.

Then there were the terrible two—Yastrzemski and Conigliaro—and the old terror of years past; the ghost of years past and seasons lost, the other Williams: Ted.

Williams the First.

It was a team which had not proven itself thoroughbred. There were some who could individually be considered such. A team must be treated individually as well as collectively. A thoroughbred must be gentled in various ways.

Williams the Second could not afford an error in judgment. He cut into it on a team basis, slicing swiftly, seeming everywhere, cocky, tough and at times even a little bit convincing while everyone who knew—I mean, the smart guys *know*—while every one of these waited for him to fall on his face.

There are several views of what happened at the first team meeting. Those who were there generally concede that this statement is the most accurate.

The scene: Winter Haven, a small Florida town happy to be back in the big league, even if it was the Red Sox, the scandalous Country Club Red Sox.

Dick Williams said:

"Look. I was here when this was a country club. I've been here and I've been a lot of other places. I'm not going to tell you that I'm the greatest. But I've been everywhere and I've done everything. And the buck stops right here with me. If you don't want to be proud, then I can't put pride in you. I'll get rid of you. This is a one-year deal with me. I can put you up in the first division. I can make you proud to be a baseball player. And I can get rid of you and I can embarrass you. You pick. From this moment on, the fine for missing curfew isn't $50 and there isn't any way to get upstairs to Mr. Yawkey. It stops with me. The fine is $500 and it sticks and it comes out of your paychecks and that means every two weeks, and if your paycheck is $500 short then you don't have to account to me. You have to account to your wife—and you just try explaining that to your wife. Because I don't want to hear about it. I saw guys lose every bit of pride they had playing on this team. I got one year—and I'm going to give you the chance to be proud."

As statements go, it was a little better than those of some and a little worse than those of others.

He followed it by explaining one other thing: "There won't be any team meetings without coaches and the manager. And there won't be any team captain this year. I don't need a team captain. I don't need a spy and I don't need anyone crying cop. I run this team. I'm the boss. You live with me, you play for me and if you screw up on me then there's one solution—as long as I'm here you're gone."

Later events would prove everything he said to be right. The Red Sox worked on a shuttle to and from the minor leagues. The front office—Yawkey, O'Connell and Sullivan—gradually came to recognize that the guy really had it and that they could merge it all together with deal after deal; good trade for a change after good trade.

The magic began right then. The charisma which makes a winner. The hard work. Taking Yastrzemski aside and explaining it all to him, knowing that Yaz—in what was to be the Year of the Yaz—at last was really embarrassed and really wanted to be a ballplayer, a player in the big league. Telling Conigliaro that *he* was the manager and that Conigliaro was really a good kid permitted to go too far astray. Reining him in and giving him a little head-running room, but control, too, as you must do with a thoroughbred. Insisting that they be in shape—*really* in shape. Talking to Lonborg and making sure that he knew at last that gentlemen don't win ball games. Only the tigers stand out there and challenge and win it all.

Taking for the first time, as well, the full measure of the *other* Williams. Later, Yaz and Williams would say that at last Yaz had listened to Ted's tips. Which was true. But also false. Because Yaz—a kid often gone wrong—has to respect the manager first. There was no room in Winter Haven for two men named Williams.

Both knew it. There had been other jams with the ego which was Ted, the last of the .406 hitters. He was a good and even a kind man; a man coming in with his Cadillac and taking old players and scouts out for a steak dinner and laughter, and giving good advice to rookies. But he was always Ted, the big one, the guy who was above it all. He *knew*. They *dreamed*. He had been there. This year, he would not be there often. Williams, the manager, would not tolerate it. There were private jams, small things, but big. There was some discussion about the value of the team playing volleyball. Then there was Ted, gone to visit the Red Sox' camps—for their minor leaguers at Ocala and DeLand. The implication was clear enough. Only one Williams ran spring training. And he was in the major league camp, a given fact which would carry all the way over to the final scouting sequences of the pennant drive and the World Series, when Williams the First would abdicate in frustration and anger to Williams the Second; and even Yawkey, finally, would say, "I got to go with this Williams."

There were many events which would transpire. There was always the element of luck. But the greatest fact was that he, Dick Williams, was up there at last. He would have a foolish training season—some would say—and he would handle the press deftly on the one hand, avoiding cliques which had ruined others (a most understandable human reaction by the writers) and answering all questions; while at the same time refusing to transport the writers in the team bus, a small, hidden factor which became more important as the team—the team, that's right, an actual team out of a country club—began to jell.

He was everywhere. Arguing. Cajoling. Fighting. Some said he tried to kill George Scott by making him play right field, a position which very nearly caused Scott a concussion. It would be said that he forced pitchers beyond their limits and ruined their confidence. He was known to issue curfew fines even in spring training—and keep them private, except for the money out of the paycheck; and what did Mama think of that? He forced and conned and did strange things, like finally beating the Mets, 23-18, in one of the most god-awful spring training games in the history of the sport, each team blowing a five-run lead in the ninth before the Red Sox finally won in the tenth—that's right, the tenth—and most of all digging in on fundamentals.

Fundamentals. Making them work for it.

On another side of Florida, Red Schoendienst, himself a man up against it, himself a man on the spot, although succored by the appointment of his deepest friend and ex-roomie, Stan Musial, as general manager—on the other side, Schoendienst was doing the same.

The guys with the big cigars who knew everything were making the line. The Cards might do it. But the price was fairly long. The Red Sox would *never* do it. The price was 100 to 1.

Everyone laughed when Dick Williams said, "We'll win more than we lose." They laughed from the certain knowledge of too many years in spring training, but they wrote it because it had the half-ring of truth, and at least this was the most colorful training season the Red Sox had in a long time. There wasn't *quite* the country club atmosphere. Anybody can dream. Right?

And so they came north. Past the old scenes of Ruth and Piersall and Ted Williams, beyond Birmingham and up into the cold weather; up to play the first games, with the Boston Marathon the only newspaper opposition, because in this year, 1967, at long last the dreaded obstacle of the Boston Celtics was no longer commanding all the space. The Celtic dynasty was over. The one year—or maybe many years—for the Red Sox was beginning.

I mean, everyone knew the Red Sox would wind up eighth or ninth.

Except this fellow Dick Williams. As they headed north he was assessing it all:

The teams to beat were Chicago and Minnesota. Chicago had Stanky—the same brattish Stanky who put the Boston Braves in there in 1948; Eddie the Brat as a player; Eddie the Con Man as a manager. Minnesota had Mele—but he was in trouble. Only Williams knew he might even take over the Red Sox. Then there was Detroit, but Williams sat on the equipment trunk and summed them up with the agreement of all his players:

"They're a drinking club. They'll blow the big ones down the stretch. Look, it seems like a dream. But you know. We can win it all."

Everyone knew better.

The Red Sox opened the season. In Israel, the jets engaged at the Golani Heights near a place called Tel Katsir. In Vietnam, the infantry ground along toward an objective unnamed and which they would give back as soon as they cleared. Hank Bauer gave up cigarettes in Baltimore and the Orioles embarked on a defense of their championship. A Japanese—as was becoming usual—won the Boston Marathon and, at last, the Red Sox opened the season of 1967.

8.

The Year of the Yaz

AND SO it began.

"The Year of the Yaz."

The one year in which a man who could become a superstar actually did. It was a greatness which waited six seasons. Once he led the league with .321 (1963). Once he hit 20 home runs (1965) and once he drove in 94 runs (1962). But the total was of little value.

But now he would put it all together, this one fantastic season which is best remembered by the tumbling figure of Carl Yastrzemski, reaching high to hold up the ball, to show he caught it; stepping in and smashing the key hit, the moon-shot home runs which won the big ones; big hand methodically clamping down to hold his batting helmet on as he swung between pitches; rising, shouting and handshaking up the dugout steps to cheer for another man and to encourage other men; smiling always, answering questions over and over again in the locker rooms without a snarl and always with patience; then going out for the next period of playing time and again making the great catch or achieving the great hit.

It was his year; yes, the Year of the Yaz.

But he was not alone. In the windup, the awards would be spread, testimony to just what did happen:

Most Valuable Player—Carl Yastrzemski
Triple Crown Winner—Carl Yastrzemski
Cy Young Award—Jim Lonborg
Manager of the Year—Dick Williams
Executive of the Year—Dick O'Connell

And almost overlooked, but of equal and deep importance, a final judgment which made Reggie Smith second in the balloting for Rookie of the Year.

An award and a plaque are sometime things. For memory books and for hanging on walls. It is the men who win them under stress who create the beautiful part of this game. Whether they ever win it again or not is immaterial. For this was their year.

It began at spring training under the drillmaster, Williams. It was not a team filled with love and cameraderie coming north. Russ Gibson, the ten-year minor league veteran who came up from Toronto, at last, with Williams; up to the big league for the first time and due to be sent down twice over the season before he caught on and hung in, was one of the first to develop the fever. He was willing to bet the team would finish in the first division. Yastrzemski and Conigliaro joined him in the conversation. "Bet we'll finish fifth or better. We'll make fourth, but bet on fifth or better," they said.

An insight into their professional beliefs.

Another player of merit said, "This Williams is flaky. He thinks he's a Marine D.I. It's going to be another long season—you just wait and see."

A late snow ruined Fenway Park's sodding process and helicopters rotated across the field, strange beasts arcing back and forth under the warming sun and under special lights at night. The Red Sox were investing $11,000 extra to get the field in shape for the opener and the Red Sox players were joking among themselves that it was one more sign that this would be another of those weird years.

Yastrzemski, the boy who would privately become proud of being at last a man, said he was not going to be a politician this year. "I was worried about being traded. When Yawkey and O'Connell signed me and said I wouldn't be traded I stopped worrying. I'm in shape. I'll do well this year. I'm not going to be the clubhouse lawyer. I agree with Williams. He called me in at camp and I spoke first. I told him:

" 'Dick, anything you want is fine with me. You want me to bunt, I'll bunt. You want me to hit and run, then I'll hit and run. You want me to bat eighth, then I'll bat eighth. You're the boss. I don't want to be in any popularity contests with the manager. I just want to play left field.' "

Throughout the season, the two men would talk very little, yet as each game went on, Yastrzemski would more and more seize the leadership, become not a cheerleader, but the true leader he had never been before.

Monbouquette, now struggling to catch on somewhere (he did with Yankees), had always resented Yaz in the outfield. "If someone hits a homer off you, he never even runs back or looks around. He just stands there. It makes a pitcher feel so damn foolish, so damned naked."

This year, Yaz would never "just stand there." He was off, running, trying and making catches of balls that were obviously gone. He was the pitchers' man.

Conigliaro was always distant with Yastrzemski. Conigliaro resented him, both as a rival and because of attitude. "Yaz never seemed to care," Conigliaro said. "He just didn't get involved. It was frustrating to be on a last-place team and see a star who didn't even care."

This year, Yaz cared. The night that Conigliaro hit the biggest home run of his life—one of the six turning points of the season, the touchstone times which made this team great—came on June 15 at Fenway Park. They strung ten scoreless innings against the White Sox and now, in the eleventh, Stanky managed to drag out one run. Conigliaro came up in the last of the eleventh, Foy on and two men out, Johnny Buzhardt working the count to 3-and-2, Conigliaro missing two straight curves, then working three balls (two more curves and a fast ball, not biting, waiting, watching). Now, Buzhardt threw the big curve, waist high, right on the outside corner and it was gone, the winning homer which first declared the Red Sox a serious pennant contender and sent Stanky stomping down the dugout tunnel, raging in his anger.

As Conigliaro came home, the first man to greet him in this swarm of yelling, cheering players was Yastrzemski, big hands out, hugging, shaking hands.

Conigliaro never again thought that Yastrzemski did not care. Neither did the team. They all saw the moment and they exchanged small talk about it—serious small talk—summed up best by journeyman George Thomas, the court jester, the funnyman (maybe even the Dick Williams type of hanging-on pro ballplayer?). Thomas said, "Everyone thought the same thing. If Yaz really cared whether Tony got a base hit then we all should care. From that time on we were all a team. Everything jelled. Everyone was more interested in how the team was doing than in how anyone individually was hitting."

Thomas' respect for Williams and Yastrzemski went far beyond the norm for a journeyman pro. Thomas felt Williams' wrath on occasion. A witty man, he committed a dumb-witted play afield, came back to the bench to hear the manager say, "You're as funny on the field as you are off. Go sit down."

And Thomas joined the cast of men who would move in and out of the famous Williams doghouse.

"But that was the way Williams' psychology worked," Thomas said. "With some guys he'd kick their butts. He let Yaz and Lonborg go on their own and be happy. He got on the backs of Scott and Petrocelli and Smith.

"The big thing, though, was Yaz. He wasn't self-centered

like he used to be. He was yelling all the time and getting the other guys to yell too, guys you never heard yell before. Not a cheerleader. A real leader. The whole thing developed until you could just sit there on the bench game after game and feel that we were going to win it, that we were going to have a big inning. It was the greatest season I ever watched through," he said with a grin.

Another view, then, of Yaz and Williams, and there will still be more. Trainer LeRoux, a past master at doctoring more than just injuries or practicing preventive medicine, opened his own rooms to Yaz and everyone else. It became a gathering place; tables to take a short nap on; a place to talk and meet and exchange ideas as the heavy rock-and-roll stations droned on—the same noisy, screaming stations which once drove everyone mad, but now were playing beautiful music (*even,* they would laugh, *even* when Conigliaro sang).

Here, in other confines, unseen and unknown to the public, Yaz worked on the younger players. Williams had Popowski to handle Petrocelli, sitting right beside him; Popowski coming in hours early for each game to be dressed and at the locker, chatting with Rico, settling him down, solving his problems and his weariness and his fears; Popowski becoming disliked by some players because it seemed as though he was not the best third-base coach for a contender and was really just a guy carried to keep up the spirits of Petrocelli and George Scott and, occasionally, Joe Foy. But Popowski was fitting into one pattern—the one slot assigned to him by the manager. Petrocelli's performance indicated that the choice was wise; and besides, even to the most callous, it did become something of a joy to see the old man finally make it to the big league.

Yastrzemski worked hard with Foy, getting awfully close to him, helping, being teased as well when Foy would say, "I gotta stay close to Yaz. He carries that attaché case with the big checkbook in it. As long as he has that I'm with him."

Yaz helped him over the rough spots and over the doghouse days when Foy really needed a lift, and helped as well with Reggie Smith. Could this have been the same Yaz? Many thought it was a fraud. But the months went on and it stayed the same. Always helping, giving tips, trying, a superstar at last; and a teacher as well, telling Smith late in the year:

"Do you mind if I give you a tip on your fielding and throwing?" And his word being accepted as Smith, who had been permitting men to get an extra base on him, learned to charge the ball faster, running, fielding and throwing all in one motion, rather than jerking the throw-off with too much on it—the attempt of the heave itself often making the ball go awry.

"He came across because he wasn't a phony," LeRoux said. "He was sincere. He didn't give the guys a pep talk as much as he would get the conversation turned toward baseball and the game at hand. Then he would just make subtle suggestions. He was never overbearing and his enthusiasm was so real it just had to rub off."

Later, looking back on it all, Yaz said:

"I could sense as the season went along that the guys were starting to rely on me. It changed my approach. I found I could talk to some of them easily about their problems and I felt like they wanted me to. This was the big thing. It doesn't do someone any good if they don't want it."

Most of all they wanted their self-respect back. Dick Williams and his most valuable player were giving it to them. Yawkey came into town early in June to see his team for the first time and became enchanted with it, calling Williams after road games to discuss it, watching it, saying by June:

"This guy has got it. He's playing the most interesting baseball I've seen in years."

By that time, Williams was no longer in trouble about extending his contract—assuming he stayed up in the first division.

Perhaps in the final sense it was because of the way he

made a player out of Yastrzemski. Yawkey's fondest memory of the year was the fact that Yaz had become a man and the owner's statement about Williams in mid-June indicates precisely what Williams' status had been previously and what it would be for the future:

"I knew about ten days after I got here that I wanted Dick back with us. It wasn't any one particular thing, but it was the way he was running the whole show. He was doing an outstanding job of being a manager, but he was also running things and—what was more important—he was also running things off the field. He was handling the men well. He had control. Nowadays, I think handling the players is the biggest part of the job. He knew how to delegate authority to his coaches, too. He wasn't the whole show. He just blended everything and made it all part of the organization."

So it was Williams and Yaz, Yaz and Williams; and around these two opposites there polarized that remarkable élan which brought Boston a run for the money—and a run for their pride.

It was not all sweetness and light. There were at least three major revolts; each of them nipped in time by a leading player or a coach or by a firm stand on the part of the manager. Reggie Smith was heard to snarl and go after George Scott when the first baseman's ribbing became too harsh: "You want a fat lip?" and really tagging for him. But that flurry died and such physical things are normal when men are under stress. Williams and Foy said unkind things to each other midway and two legends sprang from this, one that Williams definitely knocked Foy out in a locked manager's room and the other that Foy got in a good swing at Williams. Those who observed it kept their mouths shut, but the private consensus is that it was a wild scene, but no blows were struck.

There were a few other incidentals of a personal nature, including Elston Howard, who finally took Scott aside and cautioned him about his overly ripe use of a typical American idiom, but it was a winning kind of fighting, not like the old days when Stuart went after Wilson in straight racial hatred; not like when Lewis tried to cripple Speaker with the bat; not at all like the other bats which were splintered and used as threatening spikes in the locker rooms of Williams the First.

The real revolts, the ones which possibly might have gotten out of hand, centered around egos, curfews and fines and sudden trips to other teams or the minors, and it is to the credit of the front office—of Yawkey, O'Connell and Sullivan—and equally to the credit of Williams himself that this was the year when the buck stopped right smack in the manager's room. No stories were allowed upstairs and each revolt toppled quickly to best be forgotten, the lesson nevertheless to be seared inside the mind of each man on the team. There was one boss—Williams.

Now, it was time for this odd cast, this gang of losers, to start the run for it. The pitching rotation at the beginning was Lonborg, Darrell Brandon, Billy Rohr, Dennis Bennett, and Hank Fischer. No contender ever started with a weaker staff. By August, Brandon was in the bullpen, Lonborg was on his way to the Cy Young Award and the other three had drifted away; gone, baby, gone to other and poorer pastures.

The season of heroes began. The two main instruments were Yaz and Lonborg—the two men with the greatest staying power—and pirouetting around them were Scott and Conigliaro and the lighter weaponry of Foy, Smith, and Petrocelli.

It was long since the days when the NAACP threatened a boycott—Pumpsie Green was forgotten, a myth; a poor sacrifice of long ago; the Monster, with his six-pack of V.O. and his Ratpack, was gone as well; Herman was coaching the Angels; Pesky was with the Pirates; McCarthy was an eighty-year-old man living in Buffalo; Cronin was the American

League President. Higgins? Well, Hig was in Dallas, everyone guessed, although they would see him and welcome him sometimes along the road. The scales were in better balance now and they opened and began the long run:

APRIL

Opening day at Fenway, Lonborg pitched and Petrocelli hit a three-run homer to beat the White Sox, 5-4 . . . Williams said, "I'm the only chief. All the rest are Indians." The Chief then proceeded to get thrown out of a game with the Yanks by an old nemesis, Umpire Red Flaherty. People said, "Hey, the guy has color. A flair for it." . . . The Sox pitchers battled the Yanks for eighteen innings before New York finally won on Pepitone's hit, but it wasn't a disaster. The pitchers had staying power for a change and two days later young Bill Rohr went eight and two-thirds innings toward a no-hitter with Yaz controlling the second out of the ninth with a rolling, tumbling catch, the first of his many unbelievable ones. But the next man, Elston Howard, singled to make it a one-hitter, the same Howard who would come back to help the Sox down the stretch. Jackie Kennedy was among those present with her son, John ("Please don't call me John-John anymore"), and even now there was the touch, the feeling of being embraced by celebrity among the Sox. Howard said, "We tried everything on this Yaz. Nothing works. The only thing you can do is keep them up tight against him. Real tight. And hope." . . . Lonborg struck out thirteen Athletics while pitching a shutout . . . April was the month of the giveaway. No one had really jelled yet . . . At Detroit Johnny Sain—oh, remember the great Boston Braves days of "Spahn and Sain and pray for rain"; of the Red Sox losing the play-off to Cleveland for that 1948 World Series; of Sain with the Yankees jamming it down Boston's throat in three seasons of pennants and two World Series wins? And Sain, the guy who couldn't get along with Mele at Minnesota. Now he and Hal Naragon had switched camps to Detroit, the team which had the best lock on it with Minnesota and Baltimore; the team which had a reputation, but seemed to want a pennant. Al Kaline was even taking batting practice at 8:30 in the morning, smiling and answering, "Why? It's simple. I've been in the league for fourteen years and I want to know what it's like to play in a World Series." Sain was working with his pitchers, grading them, saying of Mele: "Sam and I just couldn't get along." . . . In Minnesota, Mele was getting grayer, an enormously nice, talented man without support from his front office, whose players were engaged in a game of bumble-stumble, making all the wrong plays; a team which he tried to discipline by holding batting practice for two hours after a Sunday game and by assessing fines from Tovar and Ollum for inadequate defensive play. But it was a team with Dean Chance and Killebrew and Allison and Versalles—*the* talent of the league—and the kid who would be Rookie of the Year, Rod Carew . . . It was the threat. Baseball guys said Mele would be fired soon. Baseball guys said Williams was just lucking out. The Red Sox—"Give 'em time. They'll find their level and settle right to the bottom. Mele will have this team next year." Now the crowds were beginning to come . . . Lonborg stormed down the tunnel one night at Baltimore when he was relieved . . . Glove was thrown, uniform torn off, angry words exchanged. The score was 1-1 . . . Williams publicly said, "I love to see that spirit." . . . Privately, he determined to teach the kid a lesson . . . A few days later he was in trouble, permitting three home runs and six hits in seven innings before being removed for a pinch hitter. "I wanted to teach him something," Williams said. "Now he'll understand. I put myself on the hook. So what? I'll be on the hook a lot this season." . . . Dalton Jones was already complaining about not playing enough . . . It looked like they would find their level at that . . . The record for April was 8 and 6, and Williams smiled

Carl Yastrzemski, who made spectacular catches all year, makes this one look easy as he fields it in sun off Cards' McCarver.

Going, going, gone, as "Yaz" ties into a pitch for a home run.

and said, "We'll win more than we lose." . . . And the season moved on to

MAY

Lonborg keeps on winning. The year before he had a good sinking fast ball and a bad-breaking pitch . . . He perfected the breaking pitch in winter ball in Venezuela . . . And the brush-back pitch . . . "Gentleman Jim" is throwing at their heads and people are remembering what Jimmy Dykes said: "The American League is a much politer league. Here when they throw at your head they yell 'Look out.' " Lonborg is not yelling, "Look out" . . . His reputation is forming . . . In a game with the Angels at Anaheim, Lonborg blows the ball by the Angels for eight innings, tries to get cute in the ninth. "He's too cute. He's trying to finesse them," Williams says in the dugout. "Look out." . . . Too late. Lonborg loses on finesse, 2-1, and Williams says, "It was worth it. It cost the game, but it taught him a lesson. He's the best pitcher in baseball." . . . Fans complain Williams left him in too long. Williams only smiles . . . Don McMahon walks seven men in relief in two straight games and the front office begins looking for a trade . . . The Sox beat Detroit in a doubleheader at Fenway, May 14, hitting six homers, scoring 21 runs and come right back behind Yaz' bat to beat Cleveland in a doubleheader . . . Lonborg shuts out Detroit again, 1-0, Sox beat Angels twice on Memorial Day and Yaz hits a homer on May 31 to beat the Twins, 3-2 . . . It is clear now that no one is going to run away with this league . . . The need is for a trade . . . Bill Monbouquette, once the 20-game winner of the Red Sox, once the best they had in the bad days, is cut by the Tigers, finally winds up with the Yankees after a desperate period of trying to sign on somewhere. Whitey Ford has retired. Monbo takes his place. It is important to remember. He will win some key games which take the pressure off the Red Sox—and he will beat them as well . . .

George Scott and Tony Conigliaro go over their bats as tough road trip began in August, 1967.

Baseball is a game of shifting patterns and pressures. During May as he struggles on the phone to get another chance, the aging, graying Monbo is sitting behind the screen at Fenway after a workout. Billy Rohr joins him and is mobbed with autograph seekers. "How will I get out of here?" Rohr asks. "I wish I had that problem," Monbouquette says. Shortly he is in the major leagues again and Rohr is sent down. Williams says, "Rohr has the equipment. He needs the desire." . . . People wonder about Williams and his judgment. Williams only smiles and says, "We'll win more than we lose." The record for May is 14-14. Next comes:

JUNE

The Sox trade McMahon, the relief pitcher in Williams' doghouse, for Jerry Adair . . . The White Sox have made a bad deal . . . Almost immediately, Petrocelli hurts his wrist and for 22 straight games Adair starts and hits and becomes an integral, key part in the lift toward the pennant . . . O'Connell strikes right back by getting rid of Horton and Demeter, two other doghouse players, for Gary Bell of the Indians, another key move . . . It is a game of timing as well as luck and curve balls, and Bell, as well, begins to win. Yastrzemski just keeps on rolling. Stanky tries to rattle him by calling him a "great ballplayer from the neck down" and Yaz makes three superb catches, gets six hits, including a home run, wins a doubleheader and tips his cap jokingly to the White Sox dugout rounding third; far different than the old days when Dykes blew his firemen sirens at Williams the First . . . Stanky is thrown out of two games and in Boston tells his wife to sue Tom Yawkey if anything happens to him because of the fans . . . Hurrah. Baseball is now getting interesting . . . The Red Sox show even more spirit: Conigliaro hits the big home run in the eleventh to beat Chicago again, 2-1, and in New York Lonborg gets into a bean brawl with the Yanks which spills over onto the field. The only one hurt is Pepitone. "He slipped," Dick Williams explains . . . The Sox win, 8-1, and Joe Foy—charter member of Williams' overweight club and playing an incensed game coupled with anger at the manager and basic talent—hits a grand-slam home run at the Stadium to beat the Yanks again, 7-1 . . .

The pressure is starting to grow. Detroit loses seven in a row and Kaline joins with Hank Aguirre in a private clubhouse meeting . . . Still inflamed and raging, Kaline strikes out on June 27 against Sam McDowell of Cleveland, walks back to the bat rack and slams the bat in its slot, at the same time breaking the pink finger on his left hand . . . So embarrassed that he won't even return to see his teammates for several days, Kaline finds this telegram tacked up to his locker when he does come back:

NICE GOING STUPID. HARMON KILLEBREW AND BOB ALLISON.

And the month goes on with Bell winning, becoming one of the few major-leaguers to achieve 100 wins and everyone calling him "Ding Dong" . . . Lonborg nearly gets a no-hitter, coming within five outs of it while beating the Indians, 2-1, for his seventh win. "I really wanted that," he says with refreshing honesty. "It would have put me in the national spotlight right away."

Somebody says, "Seing the White Sox win is like watching paint dry." Witty. But the White Sox are the team to beat.

The Red Sox have a 15-14 record for June and have left .500 behind them for the last time . . . People say Dick Williams is a reincarnation of Rough Bill Carrigan. No one believes he can really win it. The league guys say, "Wait until July. They'll quit then. That's when Yaz quits." Williams only says, "We'll win more than we lose" and they move into

JULY

The Cubs are fighting the Cards for the National League lead and the White Sox are still in command. Chicago is talking of a City Series. The Cubs, it is said, are the biggest surprise in Chicago since a Brink's truck with $300,000 in cash was stuck in the snow for three days and nobody robbed it . . . Stanky's "New Breed" gives Baltimore's Frank Robinson a concussion. Baltimore is out of it for good now. It will be between Chicago, Detroit, Minnesota, California and Boston. Boston? Right. Boston. The Red Sox are fifth, six games behind. The slump begins with six straight losses, three in California and three in Detroit . . . Williams has been strict with his curfew in California. He calls everyone together after the third loss and says, "Okay, no curfew tonight. Go out and live it up." . . . It doesn't work . . . They lose the next game, too. But now comes what Williams considers a major turning point. The last game before the July 11 All Star break. "Lonborg did it," Williams says. "He shut Detroit out with three hits. Otherwise, we would have been dropping toward the second division. Instead, we hung in there."

When their All Stars come back, the Sox take off on a ten-game winning streak—the first since 1951—and when they come home to Fenway 15,000 people mob the airport. It seems like they won't even be able to get off the plane. Williams says kiddingly to his son, Rick, whom he has taken on the trip, "Here, you're the most expendable. You get off and try and make the bus. If you make it then we can." . . . Rick makes the bus and the Red Sox make it with the American League . . . They have the bit in their teeth and they are running with it . . . Williams is juggling players right and left . . . Gary Waslewski is gone, shipped back to Toronto. "It was late in June," Waslewski explains much later, after Maglie is fired, commenting on the whole thing. "Yeah. Late in June. I was starting against the Twins and Maglie said, 'If you don't win this one you're gone.' Well, he was right. I didn't win and I was gone." . . . Williams is tough. Williams is cocky. Williams is winning more than he will lose, but there is still the nagging feeling that the blowup is coming. The Sox have lost ten games by one run over the last four weeks and now they start losing by larger margins. "Here it comes," guys say. "Here they go."

July is always a bad month everywhere. In Minnesota, Manager Cal Ermer is taking deductions from his players' paychecks, too. He's fined them $250 each for missing bed checks in New York and another sum for a fight in the back of the bus in Detroit. He makes the fines stick. Mayo Smith is doing the same at Detroit and Stanky is fining for the slightest infraction at Chicago. The Cards are starting to make their big move now over in the National League. In Kansas City, open rebellion is flaring—a factor which will become eminently important for the Red Sox—and the American League is also joking about owner Charlie Finley's reaction to a long home run hit by Frank Howard, which nearly hit a sign offering $3500 for such a prodigious achievement. "The next time Howard comes to town we'll cover it up," the A's say (why waste promotion money in K.C. when you're going to Oakland in the fall?) . . . Howard takes the major league lead in homers . . . But it won't last . . . This is going to be the Year of the Yaz . . . The Sox close off the month beating Minnesota . . . A strange phenomenon springs up in Boston—pennant fever. In the predominantly Italian area of the Old North Church the new system for hanging Paul Revere's lanterns is "one if by Petrocelli; two if by Conigliaro." . . . Williams is asked about the free trip to Paris he won on a TV quiz show last winter. "I bet you guys thought I'd be taking it in July," he says. "I got news for you. I'm not going at all." . . . The record for July is 19-10 . . .

And now it was the dog days of

AUGUST

A four-game series at Fenway brought only an even split with Kansas City . . . BUT . . . on the flight home to K.C. the Athletics get into their famous "incident" with owner Charles O. Finley, who fines Lew Krausse $500 and suspends him indefinitely for alleged rowdyism and drinking on the plane . . . The final split is created with manager Alvin Dark, who will give way to Luke Appling; more importantly, Ken Harrelson is also engaging in a clash of wits and public words with Finley . . . Reflectively, that was one of the few bright spots . . . The Red Sox lose three at Minnesota, getting only one run and eight hits in three games, all of this included with Dean Chance's rain-shortened 2-0 perfect game over five innings . . . Chicago is still leading . . . On August 4, Bell hits Killebrew . . . Later, Minnesota owner

Cal Griffith will say, "When Bell hit Killebrew on the arm it took the steam out of us. His arm was swollen twice its size. He went to the plate 62 times after that before he could hit another home run."

Of such things is the baseball world created . . . It is a season of beanings and a bad one will occur for the Red Sox shortly . . . Williams is steaming as the Sox stagger and holds successive bed checks in Kansas City, catching only one man out . . . He fails to fine him—perhaps from the sheer astonishment of not finding more . . . On August 10, Williams makes good on one promise. The Red Sox win their 82nd game of the year . . . Now they will at least "win more than we lose."

It had seemed such a preposterous thing when it was said in Florida. But it is going to be one of those years. Times have changed. The jumping spots are still there—Duff's in Minneapolis; the Red Onion in K.C.; Kelley's in New York—but the Red Sox attend only to curfew hour. Then they go home to the hotel. The old days are gone. Conley, Green, Frank Sullivan, now owner of a surfboard in Hawaii. Conigliaro is still baseball's answer to Joe Namath, but in a quieter way. He has learned a lot in his few years. He cuts a wide swath, but says, "I threw temper tantrums and partied. That's what any nineteen- or twenty-year-old kid would do in this situation. But now I realize what I have to do, what I owe to this team. Besides, Williams is always checking on us and there's no way that he's going to fine me."

The season—the dog days—drag on to the sounds of Conigliaro's recordings:

"When You Take More Than You Give," which he dedicates to Billy Herman because of that $1,000 fine, "Why Don't They Understand?" which is for all umpires, and "Playing the Field," which is for Tony himself.

The Red Sox have won only 8 of 22 games, but they've also

only lost a couple of games in the standings. There *is* a chance.

O'Connell and Sullivan pluck Elston Howard off the Yankees waiver list to shore up the weakness of the catchers and to shore up the team as a whole, to give them one man who has undergone the real pressure of a stretch run.

It is coming to mid-August now, and the Twins steal first place from Chicago, beating them three straight . . . Stanky grumbles, "This is the dullest club I've ever seen," inadvertently confirming what everyone has been saying about the White Sox, then really flies off the handle, closing his clubhouse even to Vice-President Hubert Humphrey, later saying, "What do I need him for? He can't hit." . . . The Brat is in full fling now and he swings after Phil Rizzuto, the Yankees' announcer, calling him an "alibi announcer, just like he always was as a player. Guys who played with him tell me he was always an alibi player." . . . Stanky livens up the dog days of August, calling Detroit's Joe Sparma yellow in the clutch, rapping too-tight uniforms and the new fashion of highly positioned stockings "sex symbols" and inadvertently confirming that he does fine his pitchers for not hitting batters by the sheer haste, length and confusion of his denial of the fact . . . The Brat is the "Bratman" of the New Breed and he is attempting to put new life into his flagging squad. Like Williams, he announced at the beginning that there was only one chief, "From the start of the season to the end, you belong only to me," but unlike Williams he is also stimulating total antagonism among his players. Williams used this method more deftly, only with the psychology of driving certain men and praising others.

In the middle days of the month, he benches Joe Foy and George Scott for being overweight, even though he loses three one-run games. Being benched is nothing new to either of them. Scott has already sat down for striking out, not hitting to right and loafing on a pop fly. This time, he explains, "it was all because of a banana split. I just went a little over the scales." . . . Or something close to that. People aren't always sure just what Scotty is saying.

The big thing is to get the luck and the timing and the right guy at the right place again. Yaz carries them through July, even in the slump, playing brilliantly in the field and hitting. Lonborg is pitching magnificently—and "hitting" as well. He has already hit fifteen opposing batters and is on his way to a record. Andrews is the best second baseman since Bobby Doerr. Petrocelli shows no sign of flipping. Smith is steady. Conig is going well.

It is August and they are not 20 games out of it . . . For the first time in all these years, it is August and they have a chance at it, nestled in fifth behind Minnesota, Chicago, Detroit, and California.

Earl Wilson, traded to Detroit two years before, makes Williams wish he had him back . . . Wilson pitches two five-hitters to keep Detroit coming at the leaders and at the same time settles defending champion Baltimore down into ninth place, a position made even more embarrassing when, after Frank Robinson hits a 440-foot triple, he is out because Russ Snyder, the base runner in front of him, passes him going back toward second thinking the ball has been caught . . . Hank Bauer takes up smoking cartons instead of packs of cigarettes.

In Cleveland, Joe Adcock is breaking water coolers watching such events as Joe Azcue actually grounding out while being intentionally walked.

Scott is back in the lineup by August 15—"Man, I'm eating just steak and eggs. They don't weigh so much"—and hits a home run while also making two exceptional fielding plays in a 4-0 win over Detroit . . . The Sox have five big games coming up at the end of the month in Chicago and the schedule calls for them to play 28 out of 45 at home down the stretch.

Then, disaster and nearly death struck. Conigliaro was struck below the left eye on a pitch by California's Jack Hamilton. The ball follows him in, wickedly slicing across the lights of the warm night at Fenway Park and thudding with a sound that takes all the toys out of this game; a sound which puts it back into perspective as a sometimes brutal, violent professional game. Conigliaro falls. Is he dead? Is his neck broken? Is he blind? Hamilton brushed him back just too close and LeRoux is racing out to work quickly, turning him carefully to watch for broken bones, ordering the stretcher, the convoy moving quickly down the dugout steps and as quickly to the ambulance. For one week, he is hospitalized; for a month, he is partially blind. For the season, he is finished.

"I felt lazy and logy," he will remember. "Usually I have quick reactions. Maybe if I was quicker I could have gotten out of the way. Usually they don't throw at my head. I had a bad habit slipping pitches when I first came up and Doerr showed me how to do it. Instead of spinning away, he taught me to duck to the ground. I should have done that against Hamilton. But I just tried to back up and the ball kept following me until it got me."

It is a small tableau, but against the tapestry of the season, of any season, it stands out. The man in white flannels at the plate. The contending teams. The stands full on the hot August night and the arc of batter against pitcher under the lights. The loss of Conigliaro is something which should end the threat of the Red Sox.

Instead, they win 7 straight and 17 out of the next 25.

The victories are just as they should be in this world of the impossible dream. Adair homers in the eighth to cap a comeback from 8-0 as the Sox rally to beat the Angles 9-8 in the second game of a doubleheader on August 20 . . . Yaz hits three-run homers in each game . . . "That ends it for California," Williams says. "That takes them out of it for good."

He is right. California is no longer a contender . . . They go west again, Billy Herman still with them, coaching now and saying of what was once *his* Red Sox team, "They were starting to roll when I had them. They're going good now. Confidence is the thing. You got to win and know how to do it and know you can do it. Then you got to go like hell." . . . Herman is calmer and smiling since he became a coach. "The thing is," he says, "the important thing is that you're wearing a big league uniform. At least I get to play more golf now. I'll retire pretty soon and live in Florida and still be young enough to enjoy it."

The man who replaced him is not as calm. He is cocky, tough, wisecracking and smoking too much. August is dwindling. The Chicago series is coming up and yes, *yes* the Red Sox *do* have a chance at it.

The Williams doghouse has a revolving door and players scoot in and out . . . Stephenson comes back from Toronto and does a good job in relief . . . Howard settles down the pitchers, but runs into an argument with young Lyle . . . Howard didn't want to come to the Red Sox, but after a long talk with Yawkey he is happy and contributing . . . His job is to watch the young ones, but Lyle shakes him off on a 3-2 count, going for the curve instead of the fast ball—the batter singling into center field and Lyle shortly going to the showers himself . . . Howard gives it to Lyle good, telling him why, with Yaz cooling them out by saying, "Sparky, you've been up for two months and Ellie's been here thirteen years —and you shake his signals off twice. Now how do you figure that?" . . . They end up laughing, but Williams isn't laughing. "We're going to teach these pitchers to get tough," he says. "Hell, it's easy to pitch when you're 26 games behind and in ninth place. They're going to face some tough games now."

On August 21, Howard singles home the run which beats Washington and rips up any pennant threat of the Senators in this preposterous year and on the 24th Monbouquette helps his old teammates by shutting out Chicago, thus creating a virtual first-place tie between Boston and Chicago.

They are off to Chicago for the five-game series and they have the touch, the confidence. They *know* what to do. They are talking in the dugout all the time now, calling the shots, winning the impossible ones, digging themselves out of holes and now . . . The kids are coming through . . . Dalton Jones is getting big hits and the Sox are dealing with K.C.'s Ken Harrelson, set free from Finley and dealing as a free agent . . . Harrelson comes high—$75,000 worth . . . It is said this salary is for one year. Actually, it is for the remainder of 1967 and all of 1968. The important thing is that he is here to fill in for Conigliaro or to play first base . . . But there is small chance of that . . . When Harrelson arrives first baseman Scott takes off on a hitting spree which lifts him permanently back to a .300 hitter. Harrelson—as is only normal in this season of abnormalities—breaks in hitting a home run his first time up as the Red Sox collide with "Bratman" and the White Sox . . . He adds some other hitting in the series and says, "I'm a student of history and history happens in up cycles. The Red Sox are on an up cycle. Everything that happens to them leads to the pennant."

Who was to say no?

Stanky rallied the White Sox to win two of the five games and knock Boston back out of the lead . . . It was heading for September now and getting wild . . . Minnesota rallied to cling close behind . . . Detroit won three straight from the rapidly fading Angels, then blew one 3-2 in the ninth and Joe Sparma—the pitcher Stanky considered "yellow"—spent the next afternoon preparing himself by listening to recorded lectures on the power of positive thinking . . . His fielders should have done the same . . . Four errors gave the win to the Twins.

Chicago or Minnesota or Detroit.

Everyone said that.

But they overlooked the matter of luck and forcing it. They overlooked another big play; another key play which would count toward the last day. It came in the Chicago series, second game of the doubleheader on August 27. In the last of the ninth, Ken Berry tried to score from third on a fly to outfielder Jose Tartabull. One of the league's fastest men, Berry came hurtling at Howard, but Howard leaped for Tartabull's direct throw, came down blocking the plate and made the tag. Umpire Marty Springstead called "Out" and the Red Sox won, 4-3. A fan threw beer in Springstead's face . . . The Sox scurried for the dugout . . . Close, safe or out, what did it matter now? They won it, had an edge in the series, 3 games to 2, and the luck was running. That one game, that one play, would stand out late in September. Now it was just another win and another town coming up tomorrow.

The next town was New York where they had played and lost a 20-inning game last trip, rallied to win the next game, close, also in extra innings on Yaz' homer . . . Yaz was tiring and in a slump . . . Guys said, "Well, there he goes. He'll quit now."

Yaz ended a streak of 0-for-18 with an eleventh-inning home run to win 2-1 in the final game of the dog days . . . August was over . . . The record for August was 20-15 . . . In Boston, Joe Costanza of WHDH-TV—now an executive, but a former traveling broadcaster with Curt Gowdy in the bad decade—suggested, "We'd better start assembling some video tapes of the key plays of the season. This thing may go. I think I hear the sound of victory."

It was there . . . in the voices of the announcers, Ken Coleman, old pitcher Mel Parnell and Ned Martin . . . It had gone on through the season, almost at times seeming as though even they couldn't believe it. Who could blame them?

It was there, though. Yes, it was. The sound, the feel of victory.

The dog days were gone. They came back to the soft days of September.

It was time for the stretch run.

9.

The Great Flounder

IT WILL BE remembered as the *Great Race.* The greatest race since ought-eight.

Four teams fighting it out to the wire.

But it might better have been called the Great Flounder.

Nobody wanted to win this one. Everyone was slew-footed, fumbling, from tension, from exhaustion, from who knows what. The simplest home run, the easiest single, suddenly became a matter for rejoicing and screaming in Boston, Minnesota, Chicago and Detroit. It was a time of giants, makeshift though they might be. At least they appeared to be giants, striding across stage center and wielding their power through the strong arms of a hit or a pitch.

Underneath it all, in the private places of their minds, even the players couldn't tell any longer quite what it was all about. The world had dissolved down to 30 days and rules; a loss column which switched back and forth; a standing which changed overnight; teams moving from fourth to first and back again while just passing through time zones.

The Cardinals had it wrapped up over in the other league. The scouts were already dispatched to observe them closely. Frank Malzone headed the Red Sox group. Ted Williams wasn't asked. Dick Williams simply said, "Who needs *him?*"

And so they began, often looking like they were four teams fighting for fourth place rather than four fighting for first.

If emotion counts, it was transferring to the Red Sox. Throughout the country that strangest of phenomena—baseball and a pennant race—had again captured the imagination of people. The Red Sox, who for years hadn't heard a cheer in a foreign town, now heard them constantly. People were saying that they were like the old Gas House Gang; the old Brooklyn Dodgers; that they were like the Milwaukee Braves the year they took on the Yanks.

But it was fascinating.

The verbiage left something to be desired. One could prefer Stanky's purposely outrageous statements. They had more color. Baseball is a game of repeated words:

"We'll win more than we lose."—Williams.

Typical.

Now, coming down the stretch, they were saying stimulating things like:

"This separates the men from the boys."—Smith.

"We're gonna play 'em one at a time."—Ermer.

Not exactly original.

But it is a game which has rules even for words. The players were more colorful. In dress, in style, in comments. Nobody was sleeping: "No, I don't have any trouble sleeping. I just take three tranquilizers and then . . ."

Their planes crisscrossed the continent, rushing in for doubleheaders to make up old rain-out dates, or single games, tempers flaring, a fight here or there, a man taking maybe one drink too many just to try to get off the hook of it all and "The hell with it, let's relax for a minute."

Steadily and methodically it ground on. The Great Flounder.

The Red Sox were fortunate that they had the few extra ingredients—the willing kids like Smith and Petrocelli; the long-range hitters like Yaz and Scott; and the pitcher: Lonborg.

Lonborg was the key. He had poise and the courage to continue to be himself—a hard-handed pitcher plying his trade. Superstitious in one sense, highly philosophical and educated in another. He knew exactly what he was and what he was doing and what it all meant, both to himself and to his team. He was the new breed of pitcher, a man willing to answer questions no matter how stupid or how often repeated, a loner in one way and gregarious in another, a man standing in a role of to thine own self be true, throwing at heads, thinking, conning batters, winning most of the big ones. Of all the aces who were dealing in this league, of all the starting pitchers who were supposed to carry it, he was the only one who did and when the month was over he had risen from the obscurity of a $16,000 pitcher to one of the most famous men in the history of his chosen game.

No one really taught this man anything. Williams pitted himself against Lonborg in a battle of personal strengths, each in his own way winning by proving his individuality. Maglie, who might once have reached him, was obviously not strong enough now. Maglie was a good man. In his time he had a theory:

"I never get friendly with anyone. I don't want to know them so well I won't throw at them."

Part of that could have been Lonborg's philosophy, carried one step further by the new breed of youth. Even of Conigliaro, Lonborg would say:

"I don't feel sorry for him. As a batter he's my natural enemy and my sympathy is with the pitcher. As a teammate I feel bad that he got hit. But it's a different game, you know. There are two sides to it—the hitters and the pitchers."

Lonborg played it by those rules—sometimes like a game of tenpins as men fell away from his throws or watching them coming up to the plate almost as though they were on a gallows walk, knowing that he might let it go at their heads. He stood out there, making the .340 hitters think that an extra few points on the average really wasn't worth the chance.

Managers never will admit that they call for a beanball. Or a brush-back. Or whatever. It's as much a part of the rules of the game as saying "We play 'em one at a time." Of course managers do. Williams did as well. He was lucky in this case that he also had a man who didn't have to be told. Lonborg had become the compleat pitcher in this season. He knew what to do.

Maglie had helped in other times, teaching him to be more aggressive. It was unkind to say above that Maglie had never helped. Certainly he had. But it had been the year before and over the winter. He had implanted in Lonborg's mind the one missing ingredient the kid needed. Now at twenty-four he was no longer a kid. He was a man and he had the pitches and he had the big strike pitch, the one you *had* to get over the plate against the good hitters.

He also had about 50,000 young girls madly in love with him as he emerged from the pack in this month of September and strode on to be the dominant pitching figure of the Red Sox; tall, handsome, soft-voiced, a killer with a baseball and yet a man who after the season ended and all the adulation and awards had come his way would do such things as spend Halloween at Children's Hospital—and insist that under no circumstances would he permit any publicity about it.

But that was later and this was now.

His fingers were blistered and his weight was down. He was exhausted from two weeks' Army Reserve duty in Georgia—during which on one-day passes he flew north to win two big games in August. But he pitched.

"I'm just using my strike control," he said. "I was 10-10 last year. So I went down to Aragua and practiced. I used to imagine that some of the guys I was playing were the big hitters in the American League. If a man had a style like Killebrew, then I pitched to him and said, 'This is Killebrew.'

"I learned that I could pitch to a hitter's weakness and that I could throw a fast ball or a curve right to the spot I wanted. And the fast ball rises pretty good, too."

The rising fast ball rose into nineteen men. No one dug in on him. "Except," he said, "the good ones. You don't scare them."

One way or another, he scared enough of them and the great race and flounder was on.

It was still Detroit, Chicago or Minnesota. Everyone knew that.

Still, there was this something about the Red Sox locker room. Accustomed to seeing relaxed losers and even an uncaring attitude before the game, observers couldn't help but notice that there was something different. "They'll fold. They'll blow it," guys said. "Hell, remember 1948 and 1949. This is the same team. Same name. Same system. Right?"

Wrong.

Yaz had it pegged right. "You could just walk in the door and tell. I could. I could look at them and tell they weren't going to quit."

Yastrzemski wasn't either. He invited Conigliaro—who was feeling pretty out of it—to put on a uniform and come back to the bench, to be part of it. He worked with a guy here and there. They were a team. Laughing, arguing, sometimes yelling at each other still and sometimes close to a fight. Hating Williams one day, but always respecting him. A team of so many opposites. Losing Conig and getting Harrelson, major league baseball's best golfer, leading pool shark, champion Indian wrestler and sometime automobile salesman. A joker he seemed, but Williams knew from his old teammate Hodges that underneath Harrelson was a very hard man. Good down the stretch.

They needed it.

Routine plays weren't anymore. The crescendo grew and the vast tapestry which baseball can be was flecked with colorful moments, ranging from the sublime to the ridiculous to the dramatic.

The losers said, "This bum I got can't hit hard enough to score Jesse Owens from third base."

The winners said, "We'll play 'em one at a time."

Johnny Sain at Detroit said it even better:

"From here on, it's hard money. Down the stretch you really earn the dough. It takes an awful lot out of you."

The Red Sox began the hard-money time on September 1 at Minnesota, challenging for the lead and blowing it because they were too nervous and edgy, allowing three unearned runs and losing, 5-4. The next day they were worse, completely shut out, and they dropped to fourth place.

Maglie had some advice for Williams, but said, "What's the point? He won't listen."

The pitchers wouldn't either. Waslewski said, "He didn't give us much advice. The pitchers pretty much went to sleep on him."

Baseball is a cruel sport. But Maglie was long-experienced under its rules.

Minnesota was running strong with the impetuous Cesar Tovar—the little kid who couldn't make it; the little kid from Venezuela—playing four different positions to carry them; showing up each day and saying to Ermer, "Where I play today, Skeep?" Coach Billy Martin snarled that the rest of them were panicking and a bunch of inept bushers.

But they plunged on.

A onetime sportswriter turned rich adman named Andy Curcio took a chance and bought a dozen tickets for the Red

Sox' last game of the season—against the Twins at Fenway Park.

Yastrzemski's moment of truth came September 5 against the Senators in Washington. He was tired and wasn't going to play. There were guys who would tell you, "Now he'll alibi. He'll quit."

Instead, he did play, hitting two home runs. "After that," he said, "my strength and confidence came back. That one game helped me personally more than any other. I found I could still do it even when I was exhausted."

The Tigers and the White Sox locked on September 8-9-10, each destroying the other, Detroit rallying to win 7-3 in the ninth after trailing 0-3 going into that inning, then losing to Joe Horlen's no-hitter. Detroit came out of Chicago shaky and wounded. Even the bus driver got lost on the way to O'Hare airport. Kaline moaned, "From the high point of my career to the low point overnight. I thought we had them on the run."

Eddie Mathews, who had been secured to aid the stretch drive, was permitted to go home to Milwaukee from Chicago for an off Monday, fell down the stairs and badly injured his hand. "I was sober," he said. "Ain't that awful? What a time for this to happen."

On September 11, Lonborg won his 20th, beating the Indians at Cleveland and winning it with his own triple.

They floundered and fought, the four teams. Kaline hit his first home run in nearly a month on September 12 to beat the Orioles. On the 13th, pitcher Mickey Lolich, who lost 10 straight earlier in the year, picked up his sixth win, throwing curves so soft that "on one of them I wanted to run up and catch it."

By the 16th Wilson—he of the 50 suits, the 16 pairs of shoes and the Red Sox antecedents—won his 21st, beating Washington. The Red Sox lost to Baltimore and the White Sox knocked off the Twins.

The Tigers were undisputed holders of first place for the first time since June 10.

Manager Mayo Smith: "This will separate the men from the boys."

Boston lost three straight to Baltimore at Fenway, which one player said was "like losing to your sister," and in Minnesota the Twins groaned that losing to the White Sox was "like drowning in three inches of water."

The Red Sox went off on the last road trip, Williams snarling at a network camera crew taking shots of his players relaxing in the plane, drinking beer and playing cards. "No . . . no . . . no. . . . I don't want people to know my players can laugh when they've lost three straight," he said, almost in a tantrum, cooling off later and taking the crew to breakfast the next day.

Williams' nerves were showing raw ends as well. His doghouse was crowded, candidates shuttling in and out. Howard was tucked away in there after a dispute with Bell, who threw a home run ball to Andy Etchebarren.

"I called for a slider low and Bell threw it high," Howard said. "I guess some people thought I called for a fast ball."

It was a pretty strong argument between them, Bell, Howard, Williams, and there were more catchers around than pitchers. Howard, the man to steady the team down the stretch, went on the bench and Gibson—the 10-year minor league veteran whom Williams brought up with him from Toronto; the kid who even this year had twice been optioned out to Pittsfield—became the starting catcher.

José Santiago, Boston's leading pitcher in 1966 and jinx pitcher in 1967, was given a chance against Baltimore, an attempt to stop the sleigh ride. He was a surprise starter and he won, 10-3, although he tired in late innings—a fact Cardinal scouts would note, for now the Cards were also paying attention to Boston and scouting them too.

"Maybe the luck turns," Santiago said. One would hope so. He had gone bad in this season because he was in and out of rotation. A guy said, "Ah, listen, poor José starts a big one in Chicago the last road trip. He goes ten scoreless innings against them and then he runs into Mike Ryan chasing a bunt and Chicago wins it in the eleventh, one to zike. So what happens? Santiago and Ryan both go in the doghouse. Listen, this thing is so full we're lucky we can field a team."

But whether they knew it or not—hated the manager or not; took out their frustrations on him or whatever—the fact of the matter was that they were a team.

If they had known, they were in better shape than some of the other contenders on that last road trip as Williams juggled and conned and hoped. They were singing at times—poorly, it must be admitted, the most notable offenders being Petrocelli and Ryan; they were even engaging in pillow fights in the back of the jet; they were telling lies, bragging, biting nails, putting up false and real fronts.

But they were a team.

Bell said, "I won the pennant for this team. When I was with Cleveland I lost two games to Boston. Right? Okay, so now I've beaten Cleveland three times. That makes plus five for Boston and so I'm the guy that wins it for us. Right?"

Ding. Dong.

They came into Detroit for another big one. George Thomas' wife had a baby. Thomas said, "She'll never let me hold it. She's seen me field."

He watched as Boston won in the tenth on Jones' homer after Yaz tied it with a homer in the ninth. Gibson led the charge the next game, driving in two runs and keeping them in there as they climbed back from trouble, finally entering the ninth trailing and tying when Scott scored Tartabull with a single after twice missing attempts at bunts (of such small things is money saved in fines and pennants made in the

Year of the Great Flounder) and then winning from old teammate Wilson when Yaz scored on a wild pitch and Scott came in on Gibson's fly.

Bell came in to pitch to Kaline for the final out. Kaline hit a wicked smash which Jones just nailed on a good baseball catch.

Bell said, "I dazzled him."

Williams said, "Give me a cigarette. I had eleven packs before the game. I ate 'em."

Boston was *up there*. First place with a good shot.

Detroit was fading. Denny McLain, knocked out by Boston, went home and sat in a chair watching TV. His foot went to sleep. He stood up and dislocated some of the toes on his left foot.

The Year of the Great Flounder.

Mayo Smith was not surprised at the news. "It's been this way all year," he said. "Willie Horton crashes the fence. So I start to run out to see if he is okay. He was fine. But I pulled a muscle in my leg and could hardly walk. Two days later Horton's about to have a fight with Ron Hansen. I ran out to break it up and Horton spiked me."

We'll play 'em one at a time.
Separate the men from the boys.
Win more than we lose.
Gimme a cigarette.
What have I done to get on the - - - - list?
He hit a lucky pitch.

The sounds of a pennant race.

They were the team to beat now and on September 20 Lonborg was blasted at Cleveland, but they still won it on homers by Yaz, Petrocelli and Andrews and Smith's single in the ninth—doesn't this team ever win in the earlier innings? John Wyatt, the vaseline-ball reliever, came out of the doghouse to get credit for the win.

On the 21st, the Indians insisted on playing despite a day-long rain, the ninth inning being delayed by showers for an hour. Jones had a two-run single and Andrews was 3-for-3 and Wyatt came in to save that game as well. (Rainwater and vaseline on the ball? It was too mercurial a combination. No one would hit that. A new law of aerodynamics may even have been applied that wet night.)

They went on to Baltimore, gaily, gaily. Tasting it now. A shot at it.

Twenty-four hours later one player said, "Now I know how the Egyptian Army feels." Baltimore beat them 10-0. Williams the juggler went back into his act, putting in Foy, Adair and Harrelson and starting Santiago, and bailed out with a 10-3 win.

They were trying to get back into first place again—who was in first? Detroit, Chicago, Minnesota, watch the ticker, it's like the stock market, it changes by the hour—and on Saturday night Yaz hit a home run to put Boston ahead 5-4, but Brooks Robinson came up to smash Wyatt's melon (he forgot vaseline and/or water) for a two-run homer. Yaz was crying afterwards. It was September 23. It looked like it was over.

But Sunday, Lonborg went six and Williams yanked him to rest him for Wednesday's game. Boston lucked out. Jones, Scott and Adair all had four hits to win 11-7, compensating for poor relief pitching.

Jones, filling in, out of the doghouse temporarily, had driven in five runs, giving him 9 RBIs in key games during this week. He would go back to the bench soon.

Williams was saying at last, "Scott is the best first baseman I've ever seen. Better even than Hodges." Scott took no chances on eating fried chicken or banana splits, however.

Yaz had said they would win 6 of 8 on the road trip. They had done it and now they were going home for the last five games of the year, telling gags, telling it like *it had been,* baby.

Petrocelli muffed a ball hit by Frank Robinson. Foy said, "Hey. Yaz wants you to bear down on Robinson."

Brooks Robinson was next. Petrocelli turned his grounder into a double play, jogged in with Foy, saying, "Which Robinson, Joe?"

Like *it had been,* baby.

Tell it like *it was,* Jack.

Now they were going home to play *Lo, The Poor Indians,* twice. Plenty of chance for rest. Let all them other guys fight and sweat.

People were trying to figure it all out. Some remembered 1948—losing the play-off to Cleveland. That brought an automatic association with 1949—blowing the last two to New York when one victory clinched a pennant.

But this was the Year of the Great Flounder, was it not? Experts compared the Red Sox of 1946 with this team. It was agreed that only Yastrzemski and Scott could have made the starting nine. Lonborg was given only an outside shot at making the pitching staff at all.

Comparisons forget certain things. Such as the fact that this was the youngest challenging team in the overall history of the American League and that it had more spirit than the team of 1946—or 1948—or 1949.

And a cocky manager.

Besides, this was the Great Race that no one wanted to win.

Minnesota settled back into a tie for first with Boston on Saturday, losing to the Yankees in a morning game at Minneapolis (a football game was scheduled in the afternoon) .

The White Sox had the best shot. Bratman and his bunch. It figured. They had five games remaining, two with the A's and three with Washington. Entering the final week, they were a half game off the top, even in the loss column. Boston and Minnesota would have to play the two final games against each other. So, Chicago would win. Right?

Right.

Except.

They never could hit anyway. They went to Kansas City. Boston lost two in a row to Cleveland at home, even Lonborg being shelled out of there. It was over. Chicago would win it by beating the last-place, disorganized Athletics, a team with an interim manager and complete dissension as well as the derision of all baseball. Instead, that night, Chicago —going with Horlen and Peters, two of the league's best pitchers—lost 5-2 and 4-0.

The next day, just to show they could also do it without pressure, they opened the final series with Washington by losing 1-0, thus clinching fourth place. Stanky called a players' meeting:

"I want you to know that if anyone lost it, it was the manager," he said.

His players agreed with him and then went on to make things complete by losing the last two games as well—five straight down the floundering stretch.

Now there were three contenders entering the final weekend. Detroit, plagued by rain, had to play California in a pair of doubleheaders. Baseball men calculated they were out. Kaline was too old to play four straight games in 30 hours. The staff was too riddled with injuries and the same problems which were known in the spring.

No, baseball men knew it was now Minnesota or Boston. Minnesota had the lead. Boston had to win two games. And Detroit had to lose two games.

It figured.

The perfect way to wind it up. Since no one wanted to win it, well, then, everyone's imagination was captured by the Red Sox. At least, *they* might do it.

Forget everything else which had gone on. All the months

of playing. All the weeks of spring training. It had come down now to one weekend. The center of baseball was Boston. Minnesota arrived on Friday. At Fenway, the players of the Boston Red Sox, the members of the 100-to-1 shot, the team rapidly becoming known as the United States Red Sox, the proprietors of the Impossible Dream, attempted to relax.

We'll play 'em one at a time.
We'll separate the men from the boys.
Gimme a cigarette.
I still say we'll win more than we lose.
Why am I in the doghouse? Why's he benching me?

The last days of the long season began. The final two games.

10.
The Waiting Time

THURSDAY AND FRIDAY were open dates. Everyone came to the ball park. The locker-room radios blared rock and roll. The joking, roughhouse horseplay of tired men with a chance to become professional sports legends reverberated over and above it. Mike Andrews threw Ding Dong Bell into a laundry cart; Bell sprawling, laughing, awkwardly trying to get out and Andrews giving the cart a shove sent it scurrying across the floor.

José Santiago, who would start on Saturday, put his right arm into the whirlpool up to the shoulder and peered at the frothing water, not saying anything.

Jim Lonborg lay on his stomach on a rubbing table pretending to sleep, then admitting, "I'm not quite asleep. But I'm concentrating. I'm lucky like that. I can cut out the horseplay and not even hear it."

Celtics star John Havlicek had stopped by for a treatment from LeRoux. Even though he had left the team there was an unwritten agreement between the Celtics and the Red Sox that LeRoux would treat older players who relied on him when possible and Havlicek, suffering calcium in his knees, needed LeRoux again.

George Scott—his gold teeth flashing as he talked—horsed

with Havlicek, offering to play him one-on-one. "You get four shots off me in ten tries and Auerbach will pay you $200,000," Havlicek said, teasing.

"Do they have to go in, or just get the shots off?" Scott asks and an argument starts when Milt Gross says, "Havlicek would have the ball away from you before you got on the floor."

Scott raises his voice in a high Willie Mays lilt and says, "More money. Raise the ante. I'll get ten out of ten. Even Russell couldn't stop me. Get the money up."

They are laughing, most of them, sitting in the room secure from the rain which falls outside; the rain which has canceled the workout; sitting, roughhousing, whatever, around the room with a big sign which Thomas put up:

"$10,000."

The anticipated winner's share in the World's Series.

Ring Lardner said war was the real World's Serious.

But what difference, really? The whole country and even the men 12,000 miles away at the war are watching this weekend. The men in this room are one-half of the actors who will strut or stagger across the stage. Some of them are very quiet. Reggie Smith let fly balls go two games in a row and resents it when a man asks him if he choked. "The sun," he says disgustedly.

The way the season has gone, men wonder. Men everywhere. Those who *know*. Is it the season of the great choke? Will it be as Ed Linn calls it: "The great groundhog race. Every team put its head up in the last week, then ducked back in the hole."

One-half of those who will decide are in this locker room at Fenway Park. Minnesota is on the way. The soft rain is falling and Dick Williams and most of his players have gone to the Red Sox Boosters' Club meeting to receive awards (blue jackets for the players, a captain's chair for Williams); going to meet very loyal fans, who formed the club without the slightest thought that on this day they would actually be hosting a pennant contender.

Lonborg sits with his own thoughts. The deep man. The strain does not show on him, but he must wonder. Even he has had trouble down the stretch.

Guys say that the Red Sox would have won it by five games if Conigliaro had been able to play. That is academic. Guys say the Twins and the Tigers were the class of the league, but that the Twins infield leaked like a sieve and the Tigers didn't have the desire. Guys say Eddie Stanky's team was just a put-on, a major league con job backed up by a couple of good pitchers who couldn't carry the load in the final blowoff with the Athletics. People talk to people. Newspapermen come and go. Players ask, "Are you gonna listen to the White Sox game tonight?" (There is still the slimmest of chances of a tie.)

Each man is finally lost in his own world; faced with the itch of having it happen, the long, dreaded afternoon and night and morning of waiting for *it*.

Smart guys were saying, "This isn't baseball. None of these teams has any style, any style like winners. They all look like guys trying to manage not to lose."

Perhaps. The old styles were gone. The Yankees were owned by CBS. The New Breed had a new style.

Baseball is a betting game. Man to man. Man to bookmaker. The final line came out Friday afternoon: Minnesota, even money; Detroit, 3-1; Boston and Chicago, 5-1. The 100-to-1 shots were getting closer, but still, they were an awfully long way off if you figured what 5-1 meant in the final two days of the great, floundering, intriguing race.

A seasoned professional writer—a man not given to love, hate, or identification with any team—said, "Whatever way it goes, the fact is that this team gave us some interest.

They've put baseball back on its feet. Made it as good as professional football. The little guys," he added, waving an expansive arm, "the little guys in jerk towns. They can identify with the Red Sox. It's like a big Walter Mitty for the whole country."

The fact of the matter is that it was. Standing there, you could feel it.

Twenty-one years after the 1946 team, ten years after the beginning of the country club teams, they were in the same room. Probably the same kind of men. It just seemed better and on Saturday and Sunday a nation would share it on television; a good part of a world would watch them through their ears and mind on radio.

It had come to this and now everyone felt it. Santiago with his arm in LeRoux' whirlpool. Lonborg, lying there concentrating. Scotty, giggling with Havlicek. Smith. Yaz. Foy. Petrocelli. Each man.

Williams held a final scouting meeting with Malzone and the other scouts—Tommy Thompson, Don Lenhardt, and Eddie Kasko. Inside men, private men, said Kasko was really the biggest threat to Williams in the future. Some remembered that Kasko had once said of Yastrzemski: "Put him with a contender and he'll be great."

What did he know?

What did make Yaz great for this one year; a greatness, an individual superability which, when it was all over, some of his own people would savor, appreciate and fear would never happen again? His own people would later say, "We'll have trouble with him in 1968. It's like any player. Or maybe it's not. But that one season—wasn't that something?"

So the Red Sox prepared to meet the Twins, Minnesota, which had beaten them 11-5 thus far in the year.

Around the leagues, new shifts, new decisions, were made for 1968. Bauer would stay at Baltimore, granted the sufferance of another try. But his coaches were fired. At Atlanta, old Red Sox player Billy Hitchcock was fired as manager of what had once been the Milwaukee Braves, the Boston Braves, the Boston Bees, the Boston Beantowners and, yes, before the American League, the Boston Red Stockings. Hitchcock had driven his dissenters to second behind the Cardinals, then tailspinned to seventh.

On Beacon Hill, under the golden dome of the Bulfinch State House—a building housing history and a legislature often called "The Golden Follies"—a member of the Great and General Court, whose antecedents were frocked, velveted men who created something called cricket, said:

"I don't know. It seems everything this noble and august body touches turns to - - - -. I don't think they can do it now."

He referred to four days earlier, Monday, when the Red Sox had returned home victorious from the road trip, victory in their grasp. The legislators—unanimous, it was said, for the first time—saluted the Red Sox and paraded the team, Yawkey, and the staff to its forum. Wise guys said that it was therefore only natural that Boston should automatically lose two to the Indians.

In bars, in plush cocktail lounges, in homes, people argued: "Why is Williams going with Santiago Saturday? He should go with Lonborg. If *we* lose Saturday then what's the point of *them* having Lonborg pitch Sunday? This Williams is flaky."

Sal Maglie, the pitching coach, said, "It's Dick's decision."

Earlier, he told Santiago, "If I were Williams, I would throw you on Saturday. *You* can beat them."

Now, Santiago came out of the whirlpool and simply said, "Pressure is nothing new to me."

Williams stuck to his plans, shifting his lineup slightly. "I'm going with Santiago because he's had more rest. He's only worked three innings this week. I'm moving Harrelson to fourth and Scotty to fifth. Scotty is going for the long one all the time now. He's batted fifth before. I'm putting Gibson in to catch because he played well on the road. I go with the hot hand."

His doghouse people—Jones, Ryan, Foy, others—complained that they wanted in on the big one. Williams sloughed it off, denying as well a story (which is believed accurate) that he had held a furious clubhouse meeting during the Baltimore disaster.

He met again with Yawkey and O'Connell and Sullivan, the stewards of his fate, the men who had made this happen and went away to fret and hope.

Minnesota came into town, fractionalized in their internal dispute over series shares for Sam Mele, embarrassing a good man for no good given reason.

Jim Kaat would start for Minnesota, it was announced. Dean Chance would go on Sunday.

The Boston players split up. Some planned to listen to the White Sox game. ("Every pitch," Scott said. "Not me. Not a single word," said Smith.)

Yaz was tied with Killebrew in the pursuit of the home run title at 43 each. He led him by four in the RBI derby and was .319 to .314 over Frank Robinson for the batting championship.

There was a chance for a Triple Crown.

And a pennant.

That night, Chicago lost 1-0. Stanky said, "The thing that hurts was losing on an unearned run. Never mind. The mouse scared the elephant. For 157 games we laughed at them. We embarrassed the whole league. I'm not going to the World Series. For me the World Series ended tonight. I'm going to Florida to the Instructional League." Stanky put a new $40,000 contract in his traveling case. Santiago went to dinner, seeking to relax, ran into Ted Kennedy and promised him the game ball when he won. The arguments raged on and on and doctors complained about the high rate of heart attacks and ulcers in New England.

Part of the price of an impossible dream.

11.

The Money Games

THERE ARE only a few times in the toy world of sports when the beauty of it all can be crystallized. This was one of them, one of the very rare ones.

For now they were poised in the final two games of the season—one ear cocked to a radio to hear how Detroit was doing (and like all professional baseball men knowing that Detroit *couldn't* do it). Each man in the white Boston suit and the gray Minnesota suit knew that these two were the big ones, the ones you love as a competitor and fear as a professional. The money games. Baseball transcended all the seasons now, all the good seasons and all the bad ones, and all the long months of planes and trains and floodlights and warm afternoon suns. These games were for it all.

For the money, you had to figure it would be Minnesota. They started off the year as the class of the league. Besides, the Red Sox would quit under pressure. Didn't they always?

Except it didn't work out that way. It is a game of luck and bounces and very occasionally a game of grace and beauty. The Red Sox were to win the seventh pennant of their history—and the first in twenty-one years—with a combination of all of these factors.

This was one time when the kids on the sandlots could

look and cheer and create idols out of men in the big league without seeing behind the façade. There were no feet of clay on this team. They may have been nervous, but they had it, now, they had the touch in this clutch moment.

Santiago pitched the first game Saturday. Friday evening, his Central American/South American teammates took him out for a good old-fashioned Cuban meal.

It was a game, this Saturday, of heroes. Santiago pitched it with his heart in his mouth. Friday night, he gobbled two sleeping pills, pacing the floor, talking with his wife, who said, "Oliva will give you trouble."

Santiago said, "Honey, they all give me trouble."

Now he was throwing in the first inning, the noise swelling over him, a sound which rumbled, roared, subsided and then screamed out again. The pitches were high. If you knew baseball, then you knew that he was not loose enough and you knew that the ball was sailing just that little bit, hanging there as Gibson—the ten-year minor-leaguer whose courage had finally carried him to the big league—stuck out the glove for a target and tried to call the right pitches, calling them low, then reaching up in desperation as the Twins plucked at the pitch and connected.

Versalles opened the game with a single and after Tovar flied out and Killebrew walked, here came Oliva—the man Santiago's wife feared—and drilled one, a solid single which scored the first run. There was only one out and Santiago was in trouble. Williams gnawed at his insides in the dugout, the calculated risk of pitching Santiago instead of Lonborg or Bell the kind of thing he might now have to answer for through a long winter of smokers and columns and second-guessing.

"But I know I have real good stuff," Santiago would say later, recounting the thoughts as he stood on the mound in the vast sea of sound. "I no worry. I peetch okay. I get the ball down lower."

Carew grounded softly to Adair. Uhlaender went for a fast ball on 3 and 1 and grounded out as well.

They went into the end of the third inning, Santiago showing that his stuff was getting better. But Kaat—the man who had carried the Twins with seven victories in September, seven money wins—was going even better.

It is a game of luck and of bounces, as well as of heart. In the third inning, Kaat threw to Santiago. Santiago, behind 1-and-2, lunged and missed, striking out. But Kaat was finished as well. "It was like snapping my fingers," Kaat said. "I heard something pop. I had enough left to get Santiago, but I started pitching to Andrews and the arm and the elbow just felt weak."

No one will ever be certain what might have happened. But Kaat was the money pitcher. And he was finished. Jim Perry came in. Santiago's pitching grew better, surviving Harrelson's misplay on Uhlaender—a long ball which came off Harrelson's glove, bounced from Reggie Smith's shoulder and fell for a one-out triple in the fourth. Santiago struck out Zimmerman and went behind Perry, 3-0, then lucked out when Perry slashed a long fly deep to center field.

In the fifth the Sox turned on Perry. Smith doubled and Williams dispatched Dalton Jones to bat for Gibson, Jones hitting the weakest kind of dribbler to Carew, the ball just reaching the second baseman. Carew reached to scoop it, easily, a soft touch play, and the ball took the funny bounce, swinging up and hitting him on the shoulder for a base hit. Santiago and Andrews struck out, then Adair flicked his bat at a fast ball, slicing a single to right. Yaz slapped a grounder to the right of Killebrew. Carew managed to get some of it and tried to throw to first, but Perry committed a sandlot kind of omission for a pitcher. *He was still on the mound.* Base hit and another RBI.

The Twins tied it in the sixth but in came Ronnie Kline —one of Minnesota's best relievers—in the sixth. Scott greeted him with a first-pitch home run, lifting the low fast ball six rows into the center-field bleachers and risking disrobing by the Red Sox as he came back to the dugout, surrounded and torn at by manager, trainer, players, bat boys and clubhouse boys.

In the seventh, the luck still ran and now they could taste it, could swing loose. The luck was running. The Twins all season long had demonstrated a complete lack of finessse or intelligence in the skill fields of covering the right base, moving to the right part of the infield. The egos which had caused the dismissal of Mele would also cost the Twins the pennant. They were guilty of the sandlot stupidities. Andrews checked his swing, hit the ball and it dribbled down the base line for a single with Kline unable to throw him out. Adair slicked a grounder which was an obvious double play ball, hopping back to Kline, who turned and threw to Versalles.

Versalles dropped the ball.

Two men were on base on "hits" which had traveled approximately 65 feet in total distance.

The next batter was Yastrzemski.

Before the game Santiago said, "Don't worry, Yaz. I won't let Killebrew hit one."

Yastrzemski said, "Deal. And I'll hit one for you."

Kid stuff. Right? Grade school Frank Merriwell.

Except.

Except, now came Yastrzemski and here went the count to 3 and 1 and then the fast ball was coming at Yastrzemski and he swung at it and it was gone into the Twins' bullpen in right field for a three-run homer, Yaz' 44th which broke the record for left-handed batters at Fenway Park previously held by Ted Williams.

That did it. Santiago tired in the eighth. Williams called him in. He knew Santiago wouldn't have it any further. All season long the pitchers had been entrusted to the trainer,

Buddy LeRoux, knowing that when they told LeRoux they were telling Williams, but trusting LeRoux and knowing he would make the right decisions.

Santiago told LeRoux he was tiring. He walked Allison and Williams came out, saying, "Okay, José. I'll go with Bell now."

"That okay weeth me," Santiago said. "I tired."

He walked off into the rolling sea of sound, the waves growing and rushing at him, an emotion he would later describe as being the most unbelievable, the most incomprehensible of his life—the shout and cry and emotion of a city long since deprived, even unbelieving; but now yelling and screaming the cry that it was, it was true, it was believable. Boston *could* win a pennant.

Santiago had bailed out of the sixth inning with the best pitch he threw in the game, a sidearm curve which Versalles popped up with the bases loaded. He struck Killebrew out on a similar curve in the fifth and a fast ball in the seventh.

But now it was the eighth and Allison was on. Bell—the Ding Dong, the choice trade, along with Adair—came in, getting them out, the final catch being made by Yastrzemski, a graceful, going-away glove grab with a runner moving on a shot by Russ Nixon (the old Red Sox catcher who had been traded in the country club days). It is forgotten now, this catch, but it was a thing of beauty; a pretty, precise execution with the money on the line.

And so it came to the ninth, Boston leading 6-2. Tovar doubled. Bell began to deal to Killebrew, working the count to 2-2, and in the dugout Williams made the kind of decision which makes a manager and a season.

"I called the pitches," he said later. "The first was a curve and Killebrew fouled it off. I called for another curve. He fouled that one off too. I weighed it up in my mind. I thought maybe Bell could throw a fast ball by him and surprise him. I knew if he didn't surprise him then Killebrew would likely hit it out of the park and tie Yaz for the home run lead. But I wanted the game more than Yaz wanted the home run lead. I called for the fast ball."

The fast ball swirled in, higher and farther over the plate than Bell had intended. Killebrew hit it monstrously far, up and over and away to left center.

But that was the end of it. Boston won, 6-4. Later, Williams said, "I guess I don't call pitches too good. But I wanted the pennant. Yaz understood. If Killebrew walks or gets on then maybe we blow it."

In the locker room, the Red Sox were beginning to sense that rare feeling of flying. Yastrzemski was promising to buy all the champagne on Sunday. The Tigers had won the first game against California to go into first place and lost the second, falling to third. The Tigers would have to win both games on Sunday to manage even a tie.

In the locker room, as well, the man for tomorrow's moment sat on LeRoux' training table. "This is the biggest game of my life," Jim Lonborg said. "I haven't seen a big one until tomorrow. Never."

In the Twins' room Cal Ermer reviewed the season and the morrow. "It is," he said, "for the whole ball of wax tomorrow."

The Saturday night dragged on. Tomorrow came, as it inevitably must. An unbelievable tomorrow for Boston, the city which had been without for so long. It didn't figure the Red Sox would win the big one. History showed they never did.

Lonborg had his own doubts. Williams' gamble had given him the necessary rest, but Lonborg "knew that people think I'm not a Fenway Park pitcher. They think I can't beat this team."

Lonborg is quiet, educated, a man who enjoys his business and his life. He shrugged at himself: "Can you imagine a guy like me being superstitious? Just the same, I'll make this a road game."

He left his apartment and went to stay at a hotel, sleeping soundly, rising with a small bag of toilet articles in his hand and walking up to Fenway to pitch the Sunday afternoon in the biggest money game of all; a $16,000-a-year young pitcher who had been throwing in the winter league eight months before, dodging revolutionaries in Venezuela; the kid who had found himself going out to earn the last day of his $16,000 salary in a final game which meant $4,000,000 net profit to his team for this one season.

It was a quiet locker room, but not noticeably tense. There were a number of minor injuries attended by LeRoux, the psychologist-trainer, who quietly commented, "Injuries show you the class of a team. The Celtics had this. It comes from extra effort."

LeRoux' factory ground on, the radio playing its wild rock and roll, the people coming and going, Yaz coming in to talk for a bit, then Foy, then Smith, the players gradually congregating and Lonborg lying facedown on the rubbing table, trying not to sleep but at least to cleanse and prepare his mind for the afternoon to come.

Williams did not have to force or con this team now. Nor did Yastrzemski. It was the money game and everyone knew it. The statements were simple after batting practice. Williams said, "I know you think you can win today. So do I. Let's go out and get them."

They went out of the locker room, not trudging down the steps with the weight of it all, but not going out gaily, either. Going out to work, some with yells and some with a quiet smile.

The scoreboard showed that the Tigers were winning 2-1 as the game began and Lonborg got two men out, then walked Killebrew—a man who always hit him well—on four straight pitches. It was a risk. Oliva took two strikes and stepped into a fast ball, lifting it toward the fence in left, with Yaz going back, back, playing it as though he might have a chance. (For this was the Year of the Yaz, was it not? He would get it, wouldn't he?) Killebrew was running, half an eye on Yaz, a little slower than he might ordinarily have run, one thought, and the ball hit above Yaz' head, coming back toward Reggie Smith. Now Killebrew started to dig with Billy Martin waving and yelling him on for home and Smith was throwing, the ball coming down and almost seeming to halt as the wind caught it. George Scott was the cutoff man and Scott made the decision to grab and throw. He pirouetted and turned, letting the ball fly toward Gibson with Killebrew thundering at him. The play would be close.

But it wasn't. The ball went over Gibson's head—a very bad throw—and the world said, "Well, the Red Sox. It's over now. What else could you expect?"

Dean Chance, a man of many seasons, a man of many parts and a man of many egos and many events, was pitching for the Twins. Chance does not lose easily. He pitches shutouts. *The big ones.* Lonborg had lost to the Twins consistently, saying to himself—and perhaps with reason—that he never did get support from the team. They were in the third inning and Chance gave nothing.

The Twins had this monstrous one-run edge and Detroit was beating California in the first game. Lonborg walked the irrepressible Tovar on four straight pitches and Killebrew was up again with two out. He punched at a fast ball, jerking it to left, and Yastrzemski had to make the big play. The ground was soft. It was a single, anyway. Yaz decided to catch it or block it with his body with two men out and was waiting for it to come.

It was another precise moment. The one that makes or breaks—trite phrase—the season and the man.

The ball came at him and went right through his legs, hitting the wall and bouncing back to him.

Tovar scored.

It came to the fifth and Lonborg was working hard, throwing his breaking pitch more than his fast ball, behind the batters a lot, not aiming for the strikeouts. (Like all pitchers, he was aware of strikeouts, but said even before the game, "I've checked the record and Sam McDowell can't beat me for the strikeout lead.")

The Red Sox failed in their half of the fifth, then Lonborg began the sixth inning, walking Killebrew on four straight pitches, throwing just *too carefully* to this one man. Lonborg could have blown it all right then, but now he switched and went to the fast ball and the assortment, catching Oliva on a called third strike, making Allison look ridiculous on another called third strike and catching Uhlaender, the big Twins batter with muscles rippling, but hitting only an easy fly ball, almost like a muscle-bound guy swinging at a golf ball.

Lonborg led off the sixth—the Thinking Man's batter—and here he was now in a soft sea of sounds; not the ruffles and flourishes of wild waves of cheering which had come before. It was the sixth and Boston was losing 2-0 and Detroit was winning the first game and it was all over. The pitcher was leading off. Pitchers don't hit. Not even Lonborg in this kind of situation.

Lonborg thought as he came up that Chance would throw him a fast ball. "Tovar is deep," Lonborg thinks. "Chance falls off the mound like I do when he throws a fast ball. I'll bunt and beat him out."

Chance threw the fast ball. Lonborg bunted, the ball hopping hard, a bouncer, and Chance suddenly coming off the mound fast, but missing it and looking toward Tovar, while Tovar looked back to Chance. Meanwhile Lonborg was on first as Tovar tried to grab it and the ball bobbled.

It was undoubtedly the last key moment in a season of heart attacks. Later, Ermer would insist that if Tovar had fielded the ball he would have thrown Lonborg out. Whatever, it is all hypothetical. The pitcher had begun an inning with a safe bunt, which is always unsettling. Adair came next, just nibbling a ball past Carew, a well-hit single which hit the right part of the infield at the right time and after attempting the bunt on the first pitch—a time-honored requisite of baseball—Williams took it off as Jones went for the second pitch. The first was a fast ball bunted foul. Jones slapped at an identical pitch for a single and the bases were loaded, with Yastrzemski coming up and Lonborg on third, grinning with his head down as he held his knees trying to catch his breath, finally straightening up and saying to third-base coach Popowski, "Well, who would you rather have up right now? Here's the ball game."

Yastrzemski knew he wouldn't get the home run pitch, the fat toss right across the center of the plate. On the second throw, Chance crossed him up and gave him just that, but Yaz wasn't pulling. He met it simply and the ball scurried into center field, a solid single, and two runs came across, tying the game, Yaz running to first with a heart and a mind saying:

"I did it . . . I did it . . . I did it . . ." The boy completely becoming the man and the leader now, making the hit which does *it* in the clutch.

Harrelson was next, working the count to 3-and-2, and Yastrzemski went with the pitch, a bounder which Versalles snapped up. But now, the same old infield failures of the Twins came to bear again. A drill is a drill is a drill.

Versalles was confused. Instead of going for the double play, he threw home, too late to get Dalton Jones. The Red Sox led 3-2 and there were still none out.

Chance was lifted (he not only was lifted, he was gone home on a plane even before the game ended, packing it in, knowing it was done). Al Worthington came in and threw a couple of spring training pitches, the first wide and the second bouncing off the catcher's shin guards, and Yaz scored what proved to be the winning run.

The rest of it? The rest of it is simply described. They had the lead, they had the taste of it, they were hitting loosely and fielding beautifully (although Petrocelli provided one moment in the ninth when he was hit squarely in the throat with a grounder). Finally there was the formality of the new legend, Lonborg, throwing the ball to the man who would beat out Smith for the American League Rookie of the Year Award. Carew swung his mightiest, but Lonborg was out-thinking him already, a pitch with so much on it that it spun off the bat, lobbing high in the air toward shortstop as Petrocelli waved his arms at people who weren't even near him, yelling, "I got it . . . I got it . . ." (which he had better had, because there were eight other men only watching, Rico was alone).

Petrocelli got it.

In the press box two writers who remembered it all—the good years and the bad—considered climbing down the screen in their haste to get to the dressing room, perhaps dropping the idea only when they saw the swarm of kids coming up the screen at them.

On the field, Lonborg was going through the supreme moments:

"It was so great. It was the first time in my life I was ever carried off a field . . . then, all of a sudden, I was terrified. They were taking off my clothes. Somebody took off my shoelace without taking the shoe."

One by one, somehow, they squirmed and swirled their way through the crowd into the locker room. The run into the dugout at a time like this is something never to be forgotten, and never really to be remembered. The sights and the sounds come at you and go away and there is really all stillness and then the pushing, bunching, shoving, bouncing off of strange bodies and a hue of varied colors and, finally, the long tunnel and the shouts and then the dressing room.

And pandemonium.

People threw people into the showers.

People hugged people.

People yelled.

People screamed.

For this is what the Red Sox had now become. Just people. Just like any other group, whether it be kids winning a Little League tournament or a man winning a big job. Just people, forgetting their involvements and their likes and their dislikes. Kidding, laughing, pushing shaving cream down necks and into nostrils, soaking wet and roughhousing.

And listening to the radio. For Detroit still *had* to lose to California in the second game.

It took a long time. Darkness came and the long lines stayed outside Fenway Park, a crowd so vast that no member of the Red Sox could have left the ball park if they wished to. The Twins departed in their bus, passing two of Boston's Finest mounted on horses, the horses turning with their tails flicking against the Twins' bus.

"Oh, I think that's a bit too much," one joker on the Twins said. "They don't have to do that."

It was going to be over. Everyone knew it now. Detroit wouldn't win the second game. Moe Berg, the interesting, intelligent catcher of the old Red Sox, the man of affairs and eight languages who was also still an old ballplayer, the man who caught Walter Johnson in Washington and Lefty Grove in Boston, smiled and said:

"Despite the undiluted duality of baseball talent today, Yastrzemski must be considered and bracketed with all the men who were great at playing this sport."

In the locker room, Yaz was covered with shaving cream and beer and throwing some of it back. Lee Stange, who would have to pitch the play-off game against Detroit, *if*, was one of the few who was quiet. The radio drowned on. Detroit was going to lose.

Detroit was ahead, but it was only a matter of time. The script doesn't change in a year like this. Everyone knew that.

Yawkey was passing back and forth through his flock, answering questions, paying a compliment here, a back pat there, a man accepted, deeply respected. It was obvious. If Yawkey ever dreamed—and of course he had, for what man had not?—then all the dreams were true now in these crystal-clear hours of victory. Yawkey answered questions:

"This is the greatest moment of my life. How much has it cost me? Oh, I don't think figures are important at a time like this. You can't figure the money. You can lose a million dollars a year with a baseball team. But how can you tell which dollar is the right one? The expenses that don't show on the field are so high. But where would we be without people to find the players and develop them? People like Bots Nekola. Imagine if he didn't find some of the kids he's found for us like Yastrzemski."

Dick Williams pranced from player to player, kissing them, hugging them, saying to Adair, "You, Jerry Adair, are a pro," as Adair limped around the locker room after having seven stitches taken in his ankle from a key double play which caused him to be spiked.

The interviews ground on and the players called, "We want George . . . we want George . . ." and George Thomas, the team wit, the man "who never enjoyed sitting through a season more" rose majestically to give forth with barbs and laughter before being submerged.

But the champagne, the domestic champagne (Great Western) waited in the coolers. Detroit had to lose. And then Detroit was losing. There was stillness and quiet while everyone listened and California had won and the champagne came out, less for the drinking than for the squirting and the dousing and the throwing into the air, and the locker room went into one of those moments which are beyond expression.

Poof . . . as in pop.

Haywood Sullivan and Eddie Popowski were sitting in Williams' manager's room as he tried to dial a call to the Angels' Rigney to thank him for beating Detroit and the conga line descended on them, picking up Sullivan and Popowski and throwing them in the shower.

The sounds can never be recorded on paper.

Only the words.

Yawkey turned to Dick Williams, borrowing a paper cup held by a writer.

"I haven't had a drink in four years," Yawkey said. "But I'll have this one with you. Here's to you, Dick."

The long night soared on. Someone said, "I always told you the Red Sox were a drinking team."

Another guy said, "Yeah, but not this way. This is the first time I ever saw them have a reason."

The Impossible Dream had come true.

12.

El Birdos

IT FIGURED that if the Impossible Dream was going to follow the script, then at the windup it would have to be Boston against the St. Louis Cardinals. Who else could it have been? In two teams the conflict situation was perfect—the old nemesis who had beaten the Red Sox in seven games in their only prior modern World Series; with Stan Musial (Ted Williams' rival) now the general manager; Roger Maris, a Yankee retread and the man who broke Ruth's record, now a Cardinal; the rich heritage of the old Gas House Gang against the same heritage of the monied Red Sox.

The perfect script. And if it didn't end properly for Boston, well, still, it at least went the full seven games and the opponent was superb, even if at the blowoff, at the very end of this Series which restored some faith in baseball, there was a genuine and strong antipathy between the two teams—antipathy, hell, it was the strongest, bitterest, deepest of dislikes—well, then, even if this were so it at least showed all the emotion and feeling and depth of two hardheaded teams colliding against each other for pride and money, with maybe for a change it being as much a matter of the pride as of the money.

The Gas House Gang was long since gone. It was *El Birdos* this year, a wry, laughing, winning, amusing group of good cheer; honest, sincere good cheer, not forced and phony.

Baseball has its three ethnic problems: whites, Negroes and those of Spanish descent. No one group understands the other completely, either in emotion or in tongue, and if the Puerto Ricans, by one example, are in one corner of the room and laughing, then it is natural that the whites in another may think that they are laughing at them.

Such has ruined more than one good team, the San Francisco Giants being the prime example; a team which had destiny in its grip, but seemed finally to be more interested in a masochistic desire to eliminate and destroy itself.

One of the ultimate moves in this had been the trade of Orlando Cepeda and now here he was in the St. Louis uniform, not a malcontent but a charming, laughing, witty man, toting around his massive collection of records and his favorite Thelonius Monk, a musician many do not understand, of which the same had been said of Cepeda's own talents.

Cepeda, with his magic potion of special honey from the high hills of Puerto Rico, was one factor. The reluctant Giant gone mad with joy in St. Louis and always delegated to lead the cheering. Victory after victory, he would plunge into the clubhouse and raising his huge right fist in the air begin the chant:

"El Birdos."

The answer came, each man on the team: *"Yeah."*

"El Birdos," it was repeated three times—the superstition was necessary, everything had to be just right for this team —and then at the end of the last cheer Cepeda would put in the zinger, turning, laughing and yelling:

"- - - - *Herman Franks."*

An ungracious, but accurate description of his feelings for his former manager.

Across the room, quiet, thin-lipped, about as tough a guy as you could ever meet when you look him in the eyes, the manager, Red Schoendienst, would smile at the holler and hooliganism; Schoendienst, who had played and beaten Boston in 1946, who had played and beaten tuberculosis as well for the Braves in a World Series, and who was now on the last year of a contract which would not be renewed unless he won.

But Schoendienst would win it all, the pennant, the Series. He could taste it. He could feel it. And *El Birdos* chanted around him feeling it as well, oblivious to all except the joy of being themselves, making up "inside" throwaway lines and such other marvelous gags as when Cepeda was asked which team he would like to play in the World Series and he answered, "Fenway Park."

It was a team that had everything, including not only heart but soul.

Here was Maris, traded away from the Yankees by Lee MacPhail and not even certain he would try again, striking it off somehow with Schoendienst and becoming the interesting, vital player and man that he long since could have been if his confidence hadn't been destroyed because he dared to break Babe Ruth's home run record. "He dared . . . he dared . . ."—was it the scream of the fans or the foolishness of Commissioner Ford Frick and his tiny asterisk or the temperament of some of the writers? Who knew? But who cared? For here was Maris now, putting life in the clubhouse as well, with the tease to Julian Javier, calling him "Hoo-li-an Hav-va-vare" in his best Spanish imitation while Javier shouted back about "Hodger Harrees" and all around them players joined in.

They were not a bunch of clowns. Do not misunderstand. They had "it" going for them this year, in a city where you are basically born with a Budweiser in one hand and an *El Birdos* program in the other and it was a beautiful sight to see, a massive recovery just three seasons after the palace revolt when poor Johnny Keane won the World Series over the Yankees and quit to go north and manage the Yankees and Bing Devine drifted over to the Mets.

It was a recovery engineered by Schoendienst and Musial on the one hand, and the players on the other, and when they put all the pieces together they had it running to perfection, a set-piece action which made them beautiful to watch; seldom, barely ever, making a mistake.

What made them the champions? Hard times. Hard knocks. Their candidate for Rookie of the Year was a twenty-nine-year-old pitcher named Dick Hughes. Their best pitcher, Bob Gibson, had a leg broken in July by Roberto Clemente's line drive. Joe Hoerner, their excellent relief pitcher, was a man who once had a bad heart attack and who coupled that with a broken toe in 1966 which nearly ruined him for good. It had a handsome twenty-four-year-old right-hander named Nelson Briles who played the lead role in a road company of *Damn Yankees* and who seemed to have left his pitching on the stage somewhere, and then bedamned if when Gibson was injured he didn't turn right around and come back as a key man. It had Mike Shannon, a fine outfielder, who had to be converted to third base—"very nearly at the risk of his life," Maris explained—and it did seem in spring training as though Schoendienst would leave Shannon spread all over Al Lang Field with the consistent daily series of drilled grounders which blistered the manager's hands and bruised Shannon front and rear. But he made the transition and became a third baseman. Javier, quiet, soft-eyed behind his glasses, said to be both temperamental and troublesome, had suddenly become *the* second baseman of the National League again and who was this playing at shortstop? Not Dal Maxvill? No indeed, not Maxvill. It was really Superman, mild-mannered, death-defying shortstop. There was Curt Flood and the larcenous Lou Brock, who would steal everything.

Finally, there was Tim McCarver, the ultimate catcher, the money player, be it bridge or baseball. He is *the* Cardinal, *the* leader among them all.

It is July and Leo Durocher is running up front with the Cubs. In baseball it is said of Leo that his interest only keeps up in the team if it is staying up there for the money. Leo is interested now and he is back against the team where he Gas Housed as a Cardinal. The Cardinals will win or lose the season right now, in this series and in the next twenty-five games against the leaders, and Leo is playing it for all the money.

The Cardinals are leading, 4-2, in the ninth and it is a bitterly hot day. "Iron lung" weather they call it in St. Louis. The Cubs have two out and Ernie Banks is taking the lead off second and Ted Savage is ready to leave first far behind and Al Spangler hits a single to right center. Banks is coming across and Savage is making the turn as Javier cuts off the throw and fires it for home, the throw slightly wide.

This is the kind of play that makes pennants. It will be forgotten in the months ahead, but baseball people will tell you that it is the big kind, like the one Ellie Howard made against Chicago.

It is the rare, perfect scene, of man against man, Savage hurtling, sliding full-force into McCarver and McCarver reaching out to barehand the ball, block the plate and now, slamming it down, full, hard, right into Savage's face.

The two wind slowly in pirouette and go down. McCarver is up first and headed for the dugout. The long winning streak which will bring a pennant is now alive. The Cubs are rapidly becoming dead. The Cardinals go on to win—*El Birdos* go on to win—21 of the big 25 from Atlanta, Cincinnati, San Francisco and Leo's Cubs.

Singing, full of life, getting help now also from an ex-Red Sox pitcher, Jack LaMabe, who left the country club on a long baseball journey which concluded at the Mets and then —surprise—moved him up to a front-runner. LaMabe had a good year all around. Revenge tastes sweetest with a world champion ring and if the World Series bonus was short, well, still, he had some other bonuses. His wife won a wine collection, a tape recorder, an electric range, a stereo set, a Pontiac and a fur coat on a quiz show; an event which outdid even Red Sox manager Dick Williams, who had done so well on his own quiz show back in the winter.

Yes, if it seems that this is a soliloquy to a good team, then it may be accepted as such. They were good. The match-up was perfect. The old legends and the new teams.

A good team from the front office of Musial down to its trainer, Bob Bauman, who would juggle everything from tape to vitamin pills in bottles labeled RBIs and HOME RUNS and who once, amidst a slump, made tomato soup, with rice. St. Louis made a quick comeback. They wouldn't go on eating the soup, but the vile concoction was perfect for dunking the warm-up ball, a superstition which later changed to painting it half-red, half-white, the ball gradually growing dirty as it was used and pitched into the dugout where only coach Dick Sisler—who had his own Red Sox memories—was permitted to catch it as Cepeda lobbed it in, one more challenge which would roll across the field at Fenway Park and at Busch Stadium.

Who is to say what it all meant? Good opposition at any rate. That at the end there was ill feeling? Well, in time we will come to the reasons for that.

Now, however, it is time for more money games. The Series. Seven full games for a championship no one really thought either team would be competing for in 1967.

13.

The World Series

IT IS impossible to call a World Series anti-climactic.

Still. . . .

It went seven games. But it was *only* the World Series, not the season of the impossible dream.

The Red Sox didn't figure to win the Series. That they did not was a pragmatic fact of baseball. In a seven-game series the best shows up on each team. Second-best is precisely that. One hates to put down the Red Sox at this juncture. Certainly, if they went seven, then the best they deserve as a footnote in the history of baseball is the fact that they were good enough to win the Great Flounder of the American League and good enough to have ambition and desire carry them the full seven against a far superior team. For the Cardinals were just that—far superior.

The one mistake of *El Birdos* was that they misjudged the Red Sox. They thought the task would be easy. The sheer desire and the momentum of the Red Sox made it difficult. But it was like the besieged holding the fort against advancing and surrounding legions. The issue was never really in doubt. It was continued day after day only by the courage of the defenders to go it to the final moment, to carry it all the way, even with the certain knowledge that it would end in defeat.

If the Red Sox had momentum, then the Cardinals had depth and rest. The two equate to a given point and then there is a breakdown. Depth beats momentum every time. The professionals of both teams recognized that going into it.

There was of course all the spectacle which goes with a World Series; especially a World Series which re-creates the scenes of twenty-one years past; especially a World Series played in a time of war and dissent.

The Red Sox came to it hungry. The Cardinals came to it poised. It was only a matter of time.

It began in Boston, back in what William Leggett of *Sports Illustrated* called the "jai alai court with foul lines" at Fenway Park.

Everyone came, of course. Wearing their various pins and carrying their various buntings, with the nation's press and some representatives from overseas. Even the Kennedys were there, the two brothers and their father, Joe, who attended a few innings. The younger Kennedys were without coats in the beginning chill of winter as the autumn shadows fell across first base. ("They *must* wear long underwear," someone said.) It was *the* place to be, this jai alai court, and there were a great many strange faces in the best boxes, so many that Yastrzemski was given to remark, "Where are all the people who were here all year? I don't recognize anybody."

Everybody was there. The *anybodys* were there, too, if in lesser seats than they had occupied during the long season.

The nation's press would fault Boston during this Series, agreeing with the Cardinals that it was "bush" and there was much ill feeling before it was over, both among fans, writers and the teams themselves. Reflectively, this, too, was only as it should be. Too long has the World Series been only a professional game. At least, this one had some fire, some fury and some taste to it.

Maybe in one sense it was "bush." But only because the people who had dreamed of it for so long couldn't absolve themselves of it in the brief carry-over period between the pennant and the championship. The Boston newspapers, always famed for their circulation wars, went themselves one better in this Series, each with *his* own writers. The *Globe* had Carl Yastrzemski, who had begun earlier in the year and even gained some national recognition from *Time* and *Newsweek* and the wire services for his accuracy and depth in reporting. Yaz' tape recordings were corrected and developed by Cliff Keane.

Cronin greets Ambassador Joseph Kennedy as Senator Ted looks on. Mrs. Edward Kennedy is in foreground, Kennedy's companion, Miss Ann Gargan, sits beside him.

Sandy Koufax and Jim Lonborg, both Cy Young Award winners.

George Scott stands on third after triple, watching sign of coach Eddie Popowski, as Cards' Shannon lands in dirt after trying to take Javier's throw. Scott went on to score.

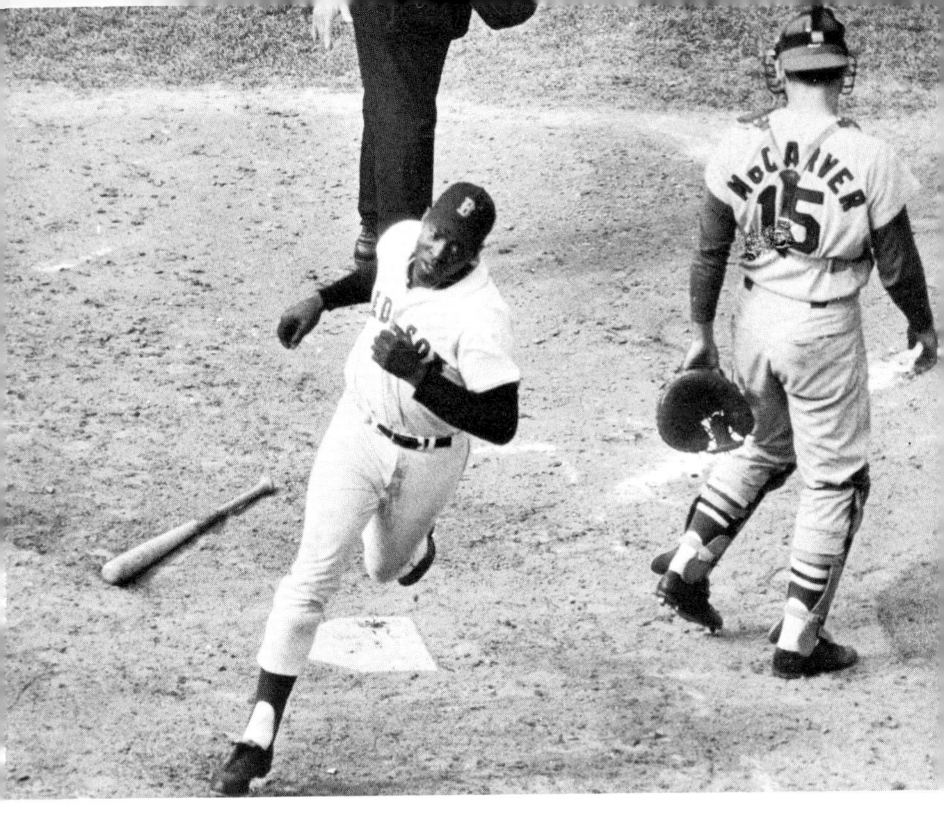

Scott crosses the plate after the ball got away from Shannon.

Brock prepares to hit as Lonborg tires in seventh and final Series game.

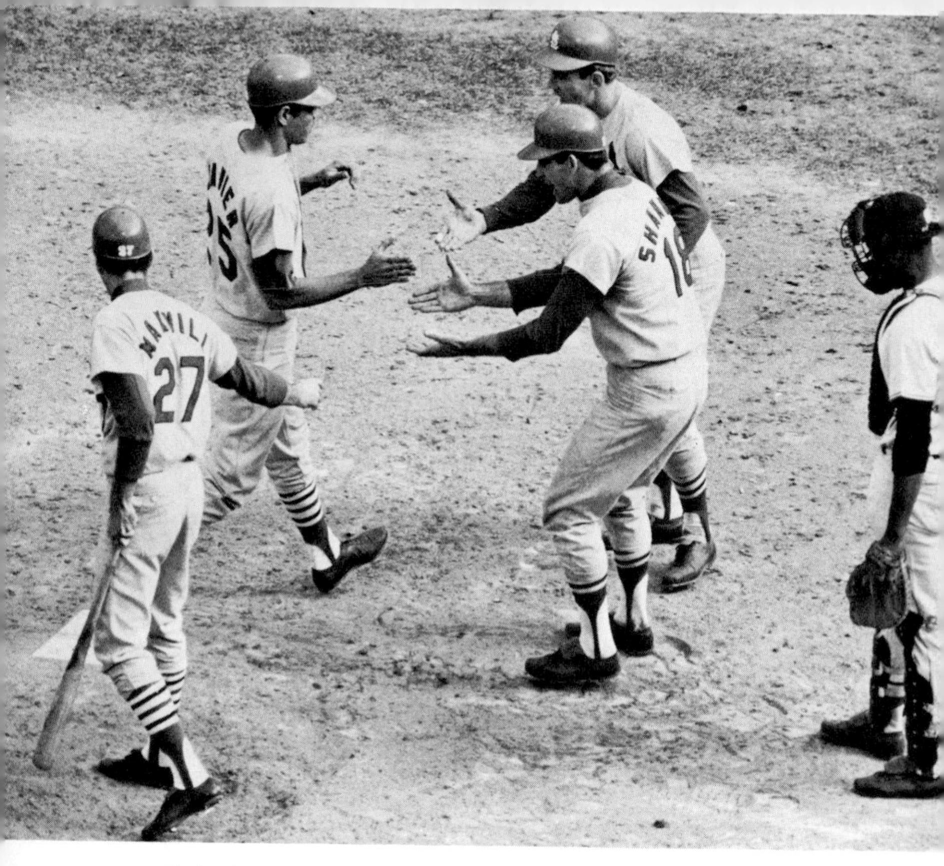

Javier is congratulated by Maxvill, Shannon, and McCarver after three-run homer, while dejected Elston Howard looks on.

This was Lonborg in form as he pitched a one-hitter in the second game of the Series.

Yastrzemski hits his second home run off Cards' Joe Hoerner in seventh inning of second Series game.

The *Herald Traveler* signed on Jim Lonborg, a countercoup of some merit. Lonborg began down the stretch and was even jotting down notes as he pitched the game which won the pennant. Lonborg's notes were transcribed by Bill Liston. The *Record-American,* not to be outdone, but late to the field, used the tactical concept of the double envelopment, with both Dick Williams (written by Larry Claflin) and Tony Conigliaro (Fred Ciampa his ghost) giving their reports.

The total effort was enjoyable and the reporting wasn't that bad. Nationally, some felt it wasn't big league. Indeed, in the final period, which we will get to shortly, there was a certain distaste and aggravation on the part of the Cardinals, who used the varied columns to their own advantage, getting steamed up, furious, angry about statements which were made under these by-lines.

Well, maybe.

If this is what it took to win a World Series, then the Cardinals weren't as good as all the professionals knew them to be. The columns were only an excuse—which is to the good, because it proves that even among the pros this is still an emotional game, perhaps even still a child's game—and if there was complaint about the columns people should have still understood one thing:

This was the first World Series in Boston since 1946.

Forgive them for being "bush." Who wouldn't have been under the circumstances? Especially when one considers that some of the "columnists" were men who began the season with incomes only a few dollars more than any average accountant or stockbroker. The Red Sox wore their fame insecurely. They had not had time to savor it. It came strangely because it was the greatest of surprises.

The Cardinals came to Boston with the élan of a team which has been to the World Series before, and, although they won the first game by only 2-1, it was a far more lopsided contest. They stung Santiago repeatedly, but the little Puerto Rican kept surviving trouble, even hitting a fly-ball homer to the top of the left-field monster to tie the score 1-1 in the third. Bob Gibson, however, is an unemotional workman. He found himself unsupported—mainly because of some superb fielding by Yastrzemski—but he played it tight and in the seventh Brock caught his fourth hit, a sharp single, then took off for second with a head-first slide which beat a high throw. Flood moved him to third with a perfectly placed grounder to the right side of the infield, one of those well-drilled niceties of the game, and Maris followed with a bouncer to Adair at second, Brock sweeping home before the throw could be made, running as he had all year on his own decision. It was the second RBI for Maris, each time resulting from a grounder to the right side which brought in Brock. Maris grinned: "You're supposed to get the man in any way you can when there's less than two outs."

After the first game, Yastrzemski led a group of Red Sox out for batting practice, hitting Joe Foy's pitches with a lovely grace, long, looping drives which settled into the empty stands for homers. It was a long way from the Yaz of the old days and it was marked down by observers. How often do you see a superstar practice after a game?

Lonborg slipped away to his hotel to keep alive the superstition that *it* was a road game and Boston prepared for game number two.

Lonborg's first pitch declared the war which would continue for the remaining games. The ball broke right in on Brock, a rising fast ball which tucked under his chin and sent him sprawling.

"You bush - - - - - -," they yelled from the St. Louis dugout. Lonborg smiled back and got the next nineteen batters in a row, before losing the potential perfect game by walking Curt Flood in the seventh on a 3-2 pitch which broke low. Yastrzemski (Gibson had said after the opening game, "He's good, but he's not the greatest") had hit one home run in the fourth, the ball falling 30 feet inside the foul line in right. Now, in the seventh, he hit another, over the Red Sox bullpen, and Boston led 5-0, Yastrzemski returning to the handshakes and bear hugs of his dugout, saying, "Thank you, thank you." Lonborg had good support in the field from Adair and Petrocelli, but he had problems of his own as well. A blister was growing on his right thumb. "I was snapping the high hard curve," he would say later. "I don't usually throw it that much. The blister started and Buddy LeRoux asked me if I was okay. I told him, 'Buddy, I have too much going right now to stop here.' "

Buddy put some benzoin spray on it.

In the eighth, he tried to reach back and give his breaking pitch to Javier. "I knew the second it left my hand," Lonborg said. "The minute he hit it I just put my left hand over my eyes like you do when you see a bad automobile accident."

Javier's hit fell for a double. It was the Cardinals' only hit of the game and now the teams flew out to St. Louis for the next three games.

Nelson Briles retaliated for the Cardinals in the first inning, throwing at Yastrzemski's leg, Yaz falling, clutching at it, then hopping up and yelling, "Thanks a lot, you——" and hustling down to first base while Williams came storming out of the dugout to protest to umpire Frank Umont. Umont called Schoendienst over. Red said something about "He didn't hit him on purpose. Pitching tight is part of this game. Besides, don't you read these loudmouths in the newspapers? They throw at us."

The tone of future games was completely set from that conversation. Williams went with Gary Bell and the Cards struck for a quick run in the first inning as Brock tripled and Flood singled him home. In the second, Mike Shannon clipped a two-run homer and when the day was over, St. Louis was leading the Series, two games to one, with a fairly easy 5-2 victory.

"We never lose on beer day," Cepeda was saying. It was part of the mystique of *El Birdos,* like their red and white practice ball. All home stands traditionally began with the delivery of an envelope which could be exchanged at a liquor store for a case of Busch products.

The fourth game was never much of an event for a World Series. Santiago started for Boston and Gibson was back for St. Louis. St. Louis won it, 6-0, with Gibson not permitting a Red Sox runner to reach second until the ninth. Brock and Gibson were clearly too much for Boston and wit George Thomas was saying, "We'll have to do it like in football and play three men on Brock."

Over in the St. Louis clubhouse, *El Birdos* were chanting the required sequence of cheers and predicting they would not return to Boston.

Some of the Red Sox privately thought this might be true. Lonborg was the choice to work the clutch game against the Cardinals' young left-hander, Steve Carlton. Lonborg had a severe cold and this would be the third big game he would pitch in little over a week. The Cardinals were still incensed over Lonborg's headhunting pitches and the Stanford graduate smiled and said philosophically, "Passion dulls the reason of all mankind. I think this is just a little matter of semantics."

He then held the Cardinals to three hits, not permitting a run until Maris homered in the ninth, and winning 3-1. Williams had gambled, packing his lineup with right-handed hitters, using Andrews, Foy and Harrelson, and although this might ordinarily have created a defensive weakness, each came through with brilliant defensive plays and created the big run of the game in the third inning.

Now, Boston was behind only 3-2 in games and Lonborg said, "We'll get them back in our green monster and it's just like when we played Minnesota."

Not quite. It still was the World Series and the little crow tracks under the eyes of each Red Sox starter showed that the strain of the long season and the Series was beginning to tell.

Williams gambled and went with his rookie, Waslewski, saying "It's going to be quite a story, isn't it?" and back at the "green monster" Waslewski did as Williams told him—"Just go out there and throw as hard as you can as long as you can."

Waslewski allowed two runs in the fourth and tired midway in the sixth, giving way to John Wyatt, the vaseline ball pitcher, whom some of the players felt has a tendency to give away a couple of runs and tie a game before he settles down and shoots for the win.

It was a home run kind of a game anyway. Petrocelli hit one in the second, then Boston went behind, 2-1. Smith, Petrocelli and Yastrzemski hit one each off Hughes in the fourth to lead again, 4-2, thus setting a record for homers in one inning and off one pitcher. Hughes gave way to seven successors, which would tie a Series record. Leading 4-2, then, along came Wyatt to serve one up to Brock, which tied it 4-4.

In the seventh, Williams sent Jones up to bat for Wyatt and Jones singled. An interesting insight into the team and Williams' style of handling them had come before the game. Jones was furious when he saw Foy listed to start at third base against the right-hander Hughes, and told Williams so. "He was unhappy on the bench. But I don't mind that. I like unhappy players on the bench," Williams admitted afterward.

"I told him I thought I was entitled to the job after the way I've played," Jones said, furiously angry, which was unusual for the normally mild manner in which he comes across. "He told me he was playing a hunch. The way his hunches have come across all year I guess that has to be all right with me."

In the seventh, though, here came Jones to pinch-hit and he singled off Lamabe. Foy followed with a double off the wall, Jones scoring as he ran right through coach Popowski's red light at third and made it easily. Schoendienst went into a relief routine, bringing in Hoerner, and the Red Sox did everything right, building up enough to win 8-4, and having all the right luck both at bat and in the field. Williams put Gary Bell in to pitch the last two innings. Bell had nothing mysterious to throw, but the luck held up, including some good catches by Foy and Yaz and, for the final out, a break in the wind as Brock's long drive streaked out toward the bullpen. George Thomas had been sent out to right late in the game and stood there, watching it come. "I thought it was going into the stands," he said. "Then all of a sudden, the wind changed and the ball stopped."

Back to the bullpen, Thomas stuck up his hand and plucked the final out from the air as a collective gasp went up.

The World Series was tied, 3-3, and people now suggested that the Red Sox could be the fourth team in history to come back and win a World Series after being down 3-1 in games, remembering that the 1903 Red Sox had done it in the first Series ever played. Fred Parent, last survivor of that team, was present and thought so, too. Up in Maine old, old Bill Carrigan—first of the great Sox managers—allowed that this fellow Williams was a good one.

Williams settled his personality problems in the locker room and the obvious was named for the seventh and final game. It would be Gibson against Lonborg, a natural, a Series game to long be remembered. Wiser baseball men shook their heads. There is a limit to the number of miracles which can be accomplished. The baseball does take funny bounces. Luck is part of any champion. But this was stretching it too far. The Cards were hitting the ball well. The bounces would have to go their way, too.

Lonborg moved back to his hotel sanctuary for the last night, knowing in his heart that he couldn't do the impossible, that he would not be able to throw with so little rest.

Williams started Foy again at third base to Jones' displeasure and the final day began.

It was completely the day of Gibson and the Cardinals and the excitement of watching Brock on the bases. Gibson gave up three hits—the last a single to Yastrzemski, who hit it in the ninth in his farewell to a superb year. Gibson was beyond worrying at that point. St. Louis had won it, 7-2.

The key moments came against Lonborg, who managed to get by the first two innings, allowing only one hit in each. In the third, his stuff seemed better than it had been, breaking down and in after Maxvill opened with a triple, and after Gibson lined to Foy and Brock popped to Petrocelli it seemed Lonborg might even get away with it. But Flood hit a soft single to score Maxvill, then Scott misplayed a bouncer by Maris which moved Flood to third. Now, the tired Lonborg tried to throw a hard curve at Cepeda and the ball bounced at the plate and went to the backstop, permitting the second run.

Baseball men said, "He doesn't have it. Williams better get him out of there."

In the dugout Williams chewed a cigarette and made the decision to stay with Lonborg.

In the fifth, Gibson smashed a home run to center and in the sixth McCarver opened with a double and Shannon hit a one-hop smash which handcuffed Foy for an error. With two on and none out, Williams went out to Lonborg. Javier was the batter and figured to bunt. "Let me get out of this inning," Lonborg told Williams. "I'm done after this inning. Let's see if I can get out of it."

It was one of those things you don't get out of. It was no longer a game of hunches and bounces. Javier—tiny, thin, wiry—went to 1-and-2 on the count and then hit the next pitch out of the park for three runs.

Lonborg finished out the inning and came off to a wildly roaring ovation from the crowd. There were tears in his eyes and his head was down ("I heard the people, but I just didn't know what to do," he said). Williams yelled some encouragement to Lonborg, but he kept right on walking through the dugout and into the tunnel as Maglie trailed him, saying, "You did your best. Keep your head up."

Later, Lonborg would say, "Dick wanted to take me out before the home run. But I wanted to pitch. I guess it's like the politician running for office time after time even though he knows he'll be beaten. He just thinks he'll eventually be successful. That's the way I felt. I knew I wasn't right, but you don't always have to be right to get the batters out."

But this was one of the times when everything did have to be right.

The Cards were the better team and now it was their luck, their bounces and their World Series.

The string played out, the innings ticking away as the Cards' red and white practice ball bounced back to Sisler in the St. Louis dugout and Williams gradually lowered his head nearly to his knees in the Red Sox dugout.

From the sixth inning on, it had been over. It was time now just for the final scenes of victory and defeat.

14.
Epilogue

IT WAS over now. The smudge of smoke was gone behind the bleachers, a last few blurs shading the darkening skyline. The wind hustled in across the freezing press box and what seemed like a full battalion of Boston's Finest, mounted on horses, pranced along each base line, warning off a crowd which no longer had the desire to dash upon the field.

A few scattered diehards had made it, one kid of perhaps eighteen stealing Cepeda's cap as he raced to the quick victory hugs near third base; being roughed a little, observers thought, by overanxious private police and the cap retrieved (what did it really matter?) and the boy turned over to the Boston police and led out up to the stands and, one would hope, not down to any station house.

The people still stood there, long minutes afterward. The dream was shattered. But was it really? Hadn't it all been impossible anyway—men from La Mancha, tilting at windmills, ghosts of the past haunting them?

Beneath, in the dressing rooms, there was silence among the Red Sox. But no real grief. Lonborg on the one flank of a line of lockers patiently answered forty-five minutes of questions, packed in, surrounded by fifty men facing deadlines, who of necessity could not hear all the answers and must therefore ask the same questions again.

Yastrzemski was pinned by another fifty, doing exactly the same thing, standing up on his stool facing them all, handling himself as well in this moment as ever he did for the money with a home run in his hands.

In the manager's room, Dick Williams sat quietly, his son Rick—bare-chested, the bat boy's uniform half off, standing behind the father as if to shelter or support a grief which really could not exist in the professional mind (but how does a young boy know that?).

Williams caught the overflow from the two men who had mainly carried them all so far; first the overflow and then gradually more and more who came to ask, to sympathize, to be *just there.*

Uneaten cakes, garnished with symbols of victory and the love of some fan somewhere, seemed to slump on one table and telegrams covered each wall, row on row of individual telegrams and just plain sheet after sheet of Telex, message after message and many, surprisingly, not just from Massachusetts or New England.

The Commissioner of Baseball William Eckert, steel-haired, trim, well-tailored in blue suit, rather hid it seemed in one corner waiting for his guide, Joe Reichler, to come back and retrieve him; a nicely sad man, it seemed, who did not belong, looking lost as though searching for an airplane or something, finally being introduced and called "Eck-hard, oh, yes, how are you, Commissioner Eck-hard?"

Joe Cronin, huge now, no longer the trim hungry kid from the Telegraph Hill sandlots, cut his wide swath through, chatting, nodding, offering a good word, belonging more, certainly, than most in this scene. A good baseball man, one thought; a good man besides, despite what baseball often demands.

Tom Yawkey came through, small for his size, wearing

the tan windbreaker and open-collared white shirt which almost made him look like someone out of the bleachers, paying his respects and condolences and moving on again while Dick O'Connell and Haywood Sullivan, the men who had helped make it possible, did likewise; not hangers-on, these men. Baseball men who knew their way around, men who had *survived* it all and could make the right moves now.

For a few, brief minutes before the crowd descended, there had been a pause in the training room of LeRoux, a closed door and four men—LeRoux, Williams, Lonborg, Yastrzemski—chatting, talking it all over, making small talk, then going out to face the final undeniable fact. It was over and it was a loser, a half dream rather than the full one.

A few disgruntled players, depressed, showing it, snarled about Williams. Mostly it was the passion of youth. "Never again. I'd never play for him again," two of them said. But why name them? Why not just say: "Settle down, kid. This is a money game. You'll play for him. Maybe you'll hate him, but you'll learn. Play it cool. Don't blow it now."

In the corner where Williams the First once hung his sign, Sal Maglie slumped in private despair, knowing he would not be back. Conigliaro, trim in suede, dressed quickly and left and others followed at their own pace, some of the older pros wisely making sure that they got everything from their locker, knowing that winter trades would be such that they would be journeying somewhere else for the next spring training.

Doerr, who had seen all the days, who had shepherded the kid Williams at the beginning, had captained the one other Series team in '46, had known it all, dressed peacefully beside Lakeman, the two men putting together what they needed and planning to move off to baseball again; moving back to Florida and the Instructional League to continue the work they knew best.

No one threw anything. No curses were heard. The long

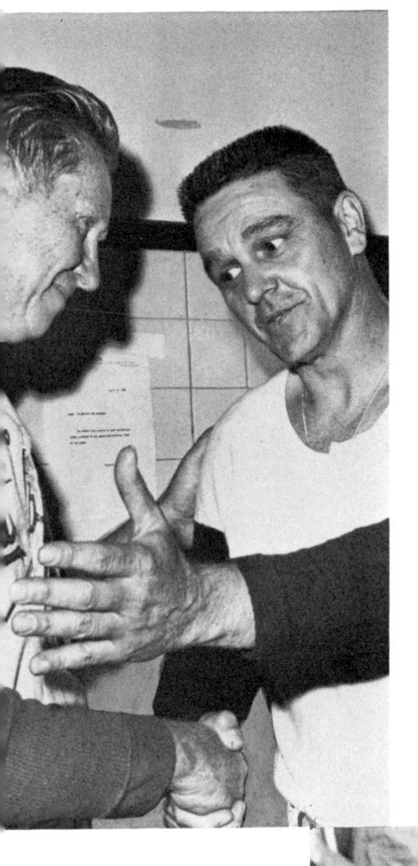

Red Schoendienst enters Red Sox rooms to shake hands with jacketless Williams after bubble burst and Cards won championship.

The Cards poured champagne with glee after winning World Series.

Waiting for the Cardinals were 15,000 St. Louis citizens

as the year of the Great Race finally came to an end.

season had ended. They went out quietly, with neither a whimper nor a bang, but with a class that an unbiased observer found becoming.

Gradually, within the hour, it finally ended and a man had a chance at last to say words to Lonborg about other matters than merely a pitched ball. He stood there tall, the towel still around his waist, and smiled and said of the year and himself:

"Well, you know. You really can't expect anything more. We gave them a great run for it. It's something to be remembered and be glad over, isn't it? At least we gave them a run for it."

They were over in the visitors' room and they with all the good reason in the world were celebrating. Budweiser gave way to champagne. *El Birdos* had every right to savor the moments. Things were said which some claimed—and this is surprising, for this is an emotional game and aren't the winners as well as the losers entitled to free expression of emotion?—but some said, anyway, that these were statements better left on the bases. An official went so far as to remark that it would be "better for the good of the game."

Yeah.

Only in baseball.

Beautiful.

But there was as much beauty in what *El Birdos* said publicly in victory. It was their right. If this had been a tough Series with bitterness exchanged on the base paths and bench-jockeying which reached extremes, than it was just as proper that reporters should describe it all.

It revolved around one chant:

El Birdos revenge:

"Lonborg and champagne. Hey!

Lonborg and champagne. Hey!"

It was less a time for splashing each other than for gurgling and it was a long conga line of passing bottles of R. H.

Mumm, bottled in Reims, France, and much better for drinking than dousing.

McCarver, *the money player,* the *indispensable* Cardinal, ticked off the savor and the reasons for it: "It was better than when we beat the Yanks in 1964. They didn't get us all excited. The Red Sox did. *They* belittled *us* in the papers," shouting it now, as though this were the most heinous of crimes, ticking off the headlines:

"Yaz Says We'll Win It in Six."

"Lonborg and Champagne."

"Scott Says We'll KO Gibson in Five."

"Williams Says Cards' Pitching Staff Is Gibson and Five Other Guys."

The taste of it all was strong for him still and the conga line wove through its chant, its taunt, "Lonborg . . . champagne . . . Lonborg . . . champagne" while McCarver said to no one in particular:

"You want more. I'll quote you every headline. They never should have done that to us. Now it's our turn to belittle them. We're the World Champions. It's beautiful . . . beautiful . . . there's nothing to compare with this."

The mood swept around the room and it was the bitterness expressed only because of victory. The man who masqueraded as Dal Maxvill, but was really the Demon Destroyer at shortstop, reached back and plucked out a beer—a man true to his owner—and recounted how it was: "They shouldn't have done it all. Knocking our wives for the mink coats. They got us so fired up Superman couldn't have beaten us. Now I got three things I always wanted—the ring, pride and money . . . and I won't even think of the money."

Curt Flood, the quiet man, said, "They shouldn't have had all that jazz in the newspapers. I've never seen anything like that in my life. Everybody had something to say. They could have finished fourth on the last day, they forget that."

Nelson Briles, boy actor, living now *the real Joe Hardy,*

could only throw his legs in the air and sprawl on a television platform and say again and again, "Oh, Mercy . . . Mercy, Oh, Mercy," and around him Cepeda pounded the beat on the platform while Javier and Jackson joined hands and began dancing.

"Lonborg and champagne."

"Lonborg and champagne."

Victory.

Musial moved slowly through it into Schoendienst's room, big grin, hand out, saying, "Well, roomie, let's have a drink. We've had a few in our time, haven't we?" And Schoendienst was grinning up at him from old memories and a joy of friendship shared this one spectacular season down the stretch when they pulled it off; pulled off the coup which couldn't be done.

"El Birdos," yelled "Hodger Harrees" from the shower doorway, chasing Cepeda—could this be the same quiet, stoic Maris of the old Yankees?—and they tripped slightly going past Eddie Bressoud, who only a few years before had escaped the Red Sox country club, Bressoud sitting there calmly, smiling at LaMabe and Muffett, ex-Sox, all three giving the same answer to the regular queries:

"Satisfying."

Schoendienst reached back to the phone and Dick Williams was on and they exchanged the right words, the proper words of professionals; meeting later, privately, for the handshake, no bitterness really between them, knowing as well that the bitterness was just part of the tension and the stretch run.

Between them, among their squads, they had made baseball a beautiful thing again. Football? Had it really started? Was it really the middle of October?

It went on and on, the quiet solemnity in one locker room, the victory of the other, but well worth observing on both ends, for it showed that this was more than just a money game. The Red Sox this year were not just paid-up members in the country club.

Conigliaro, sharp in suede, drifted out. Harrelson—the guy who came from Finley's Athletics to the big money in one short plane ride—finally stood up after sitting long with his head in his hands and began the business of packing.

Yawkey, O'Connell, and Sullivan presented themselves to the Cardinals, smiling softly at the scream *"El Birdos,"* the Cards instinctively stopping the "Lonborg and Champagne" chant; the three men of the Red Sox heading upstairs for a small, private team party.

And the beat went on, interrupted, suddenly, when relief pitcher Joe Hoerner swung a champagne bottle against a sharp edge while turning the corner of the dancing lines.

It made a sharp, bad noise, like a brick hitting a windshield, and Hoerner, stunned, was standing there with blood coming out of both hands, badly cut on the heel of the right hand and fingers all dripping blood on the left, players suddenly coming to him and Bauman, the magical trainer with the RBI vitamins and the tomato soup, rushing over with smelling salts and laying him quickly on the table.

The celebration was over. *El Birdos* began to pack, moving toward their bus, with poised Lou Brock stopping by the Red Sox room. Only Dalton Jones and Joy Foy remained with trainer LeRoux. Brock was looking especially for Smith, just to straighten out about the stolen base—no hard feelings—and just to say a word: "Good luck. You guys did well and I think you'll win it again next year."

Brock was headed for the bus now, commenting, "Our guys are excited. They don't mean all this stuff. It was the papers that got to them. I solved that problem just by not reading the papers." He had been that way all summer. Poised. Practical. Not screaming the answer to *"El Birdos"* but always the calm, watchful participant.

The Cardinals were gone to the west. The traffic jams in

St. Louis were beginning and Gussie Busch was refusing an invitation from President Lyndon Johnson to stop in Washington "because we owe it to our fans to get home."

In Attleboro, a man was dying from a heart attack after watching the game on television and in the bitter cold of the press box the last words were still being hit on cold cannons of typewriters, the teletypes punching an echo back from the dark left-field wall where someone—was it Lennie Koppett, the man on the scene, or a man back in New York?—prepared the final epitaph for the Impossible Dream, one day earlier, for the editorial page:

Here's to the Red Sox of Boston,
Home of the homer and Cod,
Where Cabots now cheer Yastrzemskis,
And Old Beantown is suddenly mod.

The last words being done, some stopped for a warming pop and in the ways of sportswriters commented among themselves. The Red Sox had a press conference scheduled for Saturday afternoon. It was anticipated that they would announce the re-signing of manager Dick Williams.

"Well," a guy said. "Don't count on it. A year ago we went up to hear that Herman was being signed again. And you know what happened then."

They were all laughing as they trailed down the steel stairs from the roof, past 10,000 torn scorecards and away from the scene which had enchanted everyone who ever believed that the impossible was just not a dream.

Appendix

RED SOX MEMBERS IN HALL OF FAME

John Chesbro
James J. Collins
Joseph E. Cronin
James E. Foxx
Robert M. Grove
Henry E. Manush
Joseph V. McCarthy
Herbert J. Pennock
George H. Ruth
Aloysius H. Simmons
Tristam E. Speaker
Theodore S. Williams
Denton T. Young

Pennant Race Milestones

MEMORIAL DAY

	Won	Lost	Pct.	GB
Detroit	26	14	.650	
Chicago	24	15	.615	1½
Baltimore	20	19	.513	5½
BOSTON	**21**	**20**	**.512**	**5½**
Cleveland	20	20	.500	6
Minnesota	20	21	.488	6½

JULY 4

	Won	Lost	Pct.	GB
Chicago	44	30	.595	
Minnesota	42	34	.553	3
Detroit	41	34	.547	3½
BOSTON	**40**	**35**	**.533**	**4½**
California	40	40	.500	7

JULY 11

	Won	Lost	Pct.	GB
Chicago	47	33	.588	
Detroit	45	35	.563	2
Minnesota	45	36	.556	2½
California	45	40	.529	4½
BOSTON	**41**	**39**	**.513**	**6**

AUGUST 1

	Won	Lost	Pct.	GB
Chicago	59	42	.584	
BOSTON	**57**	**45**	**.559**	**2½**
Detroit	54	45	.545	4
Minnesota	54	47	.535	5
California	55	50	.524	6

SEPTEMBER 1

	Won	Lost	Pct.	GB
BOSTON	**77**	**59**	**.566**	
Minnesota	75	58	.564	½
Detroit	74	60	.552	2
Chicago	73	60	.549	2½
California	67	65	.507	8

THE FINAL STANDINGS

	Won	Lost	Pct.	Behind
BOSTON	**92**	**70**	**.568**	**—**
Detroit	**91**	**71**	**.562**	**1**
Minnesota	**91**	**71**	**.562**	**1**
Chicago	**89**	**73**	**.549**	**3**
California	**84**	**77**	**.522**	**7½**
Baltimore	**76**	**85**	**.472**	**15½**
Washington	**76**	**85**	**.472**	**15½**
Cleveland	**75**	**87**	**.463**	**17**
New York	**72**	**90**	**.444**	**20**
Kansas City	**62**	**99**	**.385**	**29½**

TED WILLIAMS' CREDENTIALS FOR HALL OF FAME

Following are the lifetime records of Ted Williams as a Red Sox player, in the World Series and in All-Star Games:

YEAR	G	AB	R	H	2B	3B	HR	RBI	Av.
1939	149	565	131	185	44	11	31	145	.327
1940	144	561	134	193	43	14	23	113	.344
1941	143	456	135	185	33	3	37	120	.406
1942	150	522	141	186	34	5	36	137	.356
1943-44-45	In U.S. Naval Aviation and U.S. Marine Corps								
1946	150	514	142	176	37	8	38	123	.342
1947	156	528	125	181	40	9	32	114	.343
1948	137	509	124	188	44	3	25	127	.369
1949	155	566	150	194	39	3	43	159	.343
1950	89	334	82	106	24	1	28	97	.317
1951	148	531	109	169	28	4	30	126	.318
1952	6	10	2	4	0	1	1	3	.400
1953	37	91	17	37	6	0	13	34	.407
1954	117	386	93	133	23	1	29	89	.345
1955	98	320	77	114	21	3	28	83	.356
1956	136	400	71	138	28	2	24	82	.345
1957	132	420	96	163	28	1	38	87	.388
1958	129	411	81	135	23	2	26	85	.328
1959	103	272	32	69	15	0	10	43	.254
1960	113	310	56	98	15	0	29	72	.316
Totals	2392	7706	1798	2654	525	71	521	1839	.344
WORLD SERIES									
1946	7	25	2	5	0	0	0	1	.200
ALL-STAR GAMES									
1946-59	18	46	10	14	2	1	4	12	.304